12/03

D0686749

AMERICAN
WAR LIBRARY

★ The Cold War ★

AN UNEASY PEACE: 1945–1980

Titles in the American War Library series include:

The Civil War
Leaders of the North and South
Life Among the Soldiers and Cavalry
Lincoln and the Abolition of
  Slavery
Strategic Battles
Weapons of War
World War I
Flying Aces
Leaders and Generals
Life in the Trenches
Primary Sources: World War I
Strategic Battles
Weapons of War
World War II
Hitler and the Nazis
Kamikazes
Leaders and Generals
Life as a POW
Life of an American Soldier in
  Europe
Strategic Battles in Europe
Strategic Battles in the Pacific

The War at Home
Weapons of War
The Cold War
The Battlefront: Other Nations
The End of the Cold War: 1980 to
  the Present
Espionage
The Homefront
Political Leaders
Weapons of Peace: The Arms Race
The Vietnam War
History of U.S. Involvement
The Home Front: Americans
  Protest the War
Leaders and Generals
Life as a POW
Life of an American Soldier
Primary Sources: Vietnam War
Weapons of War
The Persian Gulf War
Leaders and Generals
Life of an American Soldier
The War Against Iraq
Weapons of War

AMERICAN
WAR LIBRARY

★ ★ ★ ★

✶ The Cold War ✶

AN UNEASY PEACE: 1945–1980

by Craig E. Blohm

LUCENT
BOOKS®

THOMSON

━━━✶━━━™

GALE

San Diego • Detroit • New York • San Francisco • Cleveland • New Haven, Conn. • Waterville, Maine • London • Munich

THOMSON

GALE

For my aunt, Audrey Bennington

© 2003 by Lucent Books. Lucent Books is an imprint of The Gale Group, Inc.,
a division of Thomson Learning, Inc.

Lucent Books® and Thomson Learning™ are trademarks used herein under license.

For more information, contact
Lucent Books
27500 Drake Rd.
Farmington Hills, MI 48334-3535
Or you can visit our Internet site at http://www.gale.com

LIBRARY OF CONGRESS CATALOGING-IN-PUBLICATION DATA

Blohm, Craig E., 1948–
    An uneasy peace: 1945–1980 / by Craig E. Blohm.
        p. cm. — (American war library. Cold War series)
Includes bibliographical references and index.
Summary: Discusses the Cold War, its origins and the resulting conflicts, including the
arms race, the Korean War, the Cuban missile crisis, and the Vietnam War.
    ISBN 1-59018-201-4 (alk. paper)
    1. Cold War—Juvenile literature. 2. World politics—1945—Juvenile literature. 3. Nu-
clear warfare—Juvenile literature. 4. Detente—Juvenile literature. I. Title. II. Series
    D843 .B563 2003
    940.55—dc21

                                             2002000434

☆ **Contents** ☆

A Nation Forged by War

The United States, like many nations, was forged and defined by war. Despite Benjamin Franklin's opinion that "There never was a good war or a bad peace," the United States owes its very existence to the War of Independence, one to which Franklin wholeheartedly subscribed. The country forged by war in 1776 was tempered and made stronger by the Civil War in the 1860s.

The Texas Revolution, the Mexican-American War, and the Spanish-American War expanded the country's borders and gave it overseas possessions. These wars made the United States a world power, but this status came with a price, as the nation became a key but reluctant player in both World War I and World War II.

Each successive war further defined the country's role on the world stage. Following World War II, U.S. foreign policy redefined itself to focus on the role of defender, not only of the freedom of its own citizens, but also of the freedom of people everywhere. During the cold war that followed World War II until the collapse of the Soviet Union, defending the world meant fighting communism. This goal, manifested in the Korean and Vietnam conflicts, proved elusive, and soured the American public on its achievability. As the United States emerged as the world's sole superpower, American foreign policy has been guided less by national interest and more on protecting international human rights. But as involvement in Somalia and Kosovo prove, this goal has been equally elusive.

As a result, the country's view of itself changed. Bolstered by victories in World Wars I and II, Americans first relished the role of protector. But, as war followed war in a seemingly endless procession, Americans began to doubt their leaders, their motives, and themselves. The Vietnam War especially caused people to question the validity of sending its young people to die in places where they were not particularly wanted and for people who did not seem especially grateful.

While the most obvious changes brought about by America's wars have been geopolitical in nature, many other aspects of society have been touched. War often does not bring about change directly, but acts instead like the catalyst in a chemical reaction, accelerating changes already in progress.

Some of these changes have been societal. The role of women in the United States had been slowly changing, but World War II put thousands into the workforce and into uniform. They might have gone back to being housewives after the war, but equality, once experienced, would not be forgotten.

Likewise, wars have accelerated technological change. The necessity for faster airplanes and a more destructive bomb led to the development of jet planes and nuclear energy. Artificial fibers developed for parachutes in the 1940s were used in the clothing of the 1950s.

Lucent Books' American War Library covers key wars in the development of the nation. Each war is covered in several volumes, to allow for more detail, context, and to provide volumes on often neglected subjects, such as the kamikazes of World War II, or weapons used in the Civil War. As with all Lucent Books, notes, annotated bibliographies, and appendixes such as glossaries give students a launching point for further research. In addition, sidebars and archival photographs enhance the text. Together, each volume in The American War Library will aid students in understanding how America's wars have shaped and changed its politics, economics, and society.

A Conflict of Ideas

By September 1945, World War II was finally over. Hitler had committed suicide amid the rubble of his collapsed Nazi Third Reich, and Imperial Japan had been pounded into submission by the atomic bomb. Triumphant Allied armies celebrated their victories with hugs and cries of joy. After six years of war, people could now look forward to life in the postwar world. But they wondered what kind of world it would be. The form of that world would be shaped by two great superpowers, the United States and the Soviet Union. The two nations had been allies in the conflict that had just ended. Could they remain allies in the years to come?

The question was immediately troubling, for each superpower had a very different political and economic outlook and vision for the future. A capitalist, democratic society, such as the United States, is based on the private ownership of property, industrial production, and distribution of the goods and services that the nation provides. Free enterprise and the marketplace determine the success or failure of a business venture, and even an ordinary person can aspire to wealth. Governmental authority is divided to keep state power in check, and a multiparty system of free elections gives political control to the people. The government guarantees individual rights and freedom.

In a Communist society, however, the concept of private property does not exist. The state owns the means of production, such as factories and farms, and workers labor not for themselves but for the state. Property is not owned by individuals but held in common for the good of all people, and distribution of goods is based on a principle stated by Karl Marx, the German philosopher who set forth the basic tenets of communism: "from each according to his ability, to each according to his needs."[1] To achieve this economic state, Marx said, a nation's working class would rise up and overthrow its capitalist oppressors. A Communist government is totalitarian; power is concentrated in the state, controlled solely by the Communist Party. State authority supplants individual rights, until some undetermined future time when the state decides that the people are ready to assume power.

For two such clearly opposite ideologies to peacefully coexist in the postwar

German philosopher Karl Marx developed the basic principles of communism.

world was, perhaps, too much to hope for. World War II had barely ended when the Soviet Union, the world's leading Communist nation, began imposing its control over the countries of Eastern Europe. In response, the United States instituted a policy known as "containment" in an effort to stem the Communist tide. A line was soon drawn between the free and Communist societies of Europe, a line that former British prime minister Winston Churchill called the Iron Curtain. That curtain would not be lifted for forty-five years, and the entire world would become the arena in which each superpower struggled for dominance.

The conflict between the United States and the Soviet Union that spanned those years is known as the Cold War. It was a period of uneasy peace punctuated by two "hot" wars in Asia, a hunt for Communists in U.S. government and industry, and a race to develop weapons of mass destruction that threatened the safety of the world. Occasionally during the Cold War, the superpowers were able to exercise limited cooperation, such as the joint U.S.-Soviet space mission conducted in 1975. But at other times, mutual animosity threatened to bring the world to the brink of destruction, as during the 1962 Cuban Missile Crisis. This continual fluctuation between peacefulness and hostility created an underlying atmosphere of anxiety and uncertainty that defined the decades of the Cold War.

A World War II-era atomic bomb. The race to develop weapons of even greater destructive power intensified during the Cold War.

The Cold War was complex because it encompassed the grand themes of politics, sociology, economics, and science, while at the same time profoundly affecting the everyday lives of ordinary people. It was an important time in U.S. history for it molded the thoughts and actions of two generations of Americans who lived through it. But more than that, the Cold War molded the world in which we now live and will surely have an influence on future generations.

Chapter 1

Origins of the Cold War

In the spring of 1945, World War II was grinding slowly toward its inevitable conclusion in Europe. Units of the Soviet Union's massive Red Army were advancing through the German countryside toward Berlin, Nazi dictator Adolf Hitler's capital. For weeks the city had been pounded by Allied bombing raids, a devastating aerial barrage that turned three-quarters of Berlin into smoking rubble. Hitler's Third Reich was doomed, as was the man himself: He would commit suicide as Russian troops pushed toward the fortified underground bunker that was his headquarters.

While the main Soviet force was closing in on Berlin, some fifty miles to the southwest, the U.S. First Army was marching eastward toward the Elbe, a river that flows through Central Europe to the North Sea. At the river the American soldiers planned to link up with their allies, Soviet troops who had arrived there on April 23. For two days tentative radio contacts were made between the armies, but no meeting occurred. Then on April 25, 1945, two patrols of Soviet and American soldiers met in the middle of a partially destroyed bridge over the Elbe. With smiles, handshakes, and hugs, East and West had finally come together, partners in defeating the Nazi threat to the world. Unfortunately, the partnership was already beginning to unravel.

A Meeting at Yalta

On the coast of Russia's (now Ukraine's) Crimean Peninsula lies the city of Yalta, a picturesque resort at the edge of the Black Sea. It was once an exclusive vacation spot for the czars of Russia, with lavish palaces lining its beautiful seacoast. By the final year of World War II, however, much of Yalta lay in ruins, a victim of German bombs. Despite the destruction, in February 1945 Yalta played host to one of the most important conferences of the war. The leaders of the Allied Big Three nations—U.S. president Franklin D. Roosevelt. Britain's prime minister Winston Churchill, and Soviet premier Joseph Stalin—would discuss at Yalta the postwar fate of Europe. They would also sow the seeds of a great ideological conflict that would last almost fifty years: the Cold War.

It took months of negotiations simply to decide where the three leaders would meet. Yalta was finally chosen because Stalin, complaining of ill health, said his doctors advised him against any long-distance travel. American officials who understood Stalin surmised that the Soviet dictator, notoriously suspicious of plots against him, was afraid to leave Soviet territory. President Roosevelt's own declining health made traveling to Yalta dangerous. Afflicted with serious cardiovascular disease, Roosevelt would live for only two months after the Yalta Conference. But the meeting was set to begin on February 4, 1945, and Roosevelt made the long trip by sea and air despite his frail condition.

Winston Churchill, Franklin Roosevelt, and Joseph Stalin (seated, from left) pictured at Yalta.

Stalin (left) and Churchill pose for a photographer at Livadia Palace during the Yalta conference.

Meeting at Livadia Palace, once the summer home of Czar Nicholas II, Roosevelt, Churchill, and Stalin debated the fate of Germany. They finally agreed that Germany should unconditionally surrender and be demilitarized, that war crimes trials of Nazi leaders would be held, and that Germany would be partitioned into four occupation zones, with four nations—the United States, Great Britain, France, and the Soviet Union—overseeing the partitions. In addition, the leaders also agreed to proceed with the formation of the United Nations, an international organization designed to promote world peace. The Yalta Conference also included several secret deals. Stalin pledged to enter the war against Japan in exchange for territorial gains in the Far East. He demanded war reparations from

Germany to rebuild Soviet industry and special representation for the Soviet Union in the United Nations. The most controversial secret deal, however, was the establishment of Poland's postwar government and borders.

The future of Poland, as well as that of other Eastern European nations, was the most difficult issue at Yalta. Roosevelt and Churchill wanted to ensure an independent government in Poland. Great Britain, especially, had an important reason for wanting a free Poland; it was the German invasion of Poland that drew Britain into the war. Winston Churchill told Stalin, "I want the Poles to have a home in Europe and to be free to live their own lives there. . . . This is what we went to war against Germany for—that Poland should be free and sovereign."[2] But Stalin insisted that Poland posed a security risk to his nation. "For Russia," he said, "it is not only a question of honor but of security. . . . During the last thirty years our German enemy has passed through this corridor twice."[3] Ultimately, the Big Three leaders signed the Declaration on Liberated Europe, an agreement designed to assure the countries of Eastern Europe, including Poland, the ability to establish their own forms of government by holding free elections.

After the Yalta Conference, Roosevelt jubilantly returned to the United States. He was encouraged by Russia's pledge to join the war against Japan and Stalin's agreement to allow European self-determination.

But even though Joseph Stalin had signed the Declaration on Liberated Europe, his intentions were very different.

The Problem with Poland

On April 12, 1945, an America on the verge of winning World War II received shocking news: President Roosevelt was dead. Radio, the medium that had brought Roosevelt's "fireside chats" into millions of American homes, carried the grim news. "We interrupt this program," intoned reporter John Daly, "to bring you a special bulletin from CBS World News. A press association has just announced that President Roosevelt is dead."[4] Vice President Harry S. Truman became the thirty-third president of the United States, and the first to confront the issues of the Cold War. The new president was given a secret report, originally prepared for Roosevelt, that disclosed the Soviet Union's plans to dominate Eastern Europe. This was most evident in Poland, where Russian troops had liberated the country from the Nazis. Soon after the liberation, Stalin had ended the possibility of free elections and installed a Communist government in Poland. "We now have ample proof," Truman read in the report, "that the Soviet government views all matters from the viewpoint of their own selfish interest. . . . We must clearly recognize that the Soviet program is the establishment of totalitarianism, ending personal liberty and democracy as we know and respect it."[5]

President Harry Truman. His condemnation of Soviet actions in Poland stunned the Soviet foreign minister.

It would not take long for Truman, a plain-talking Midwesterner, to set the tone for U.S. dealings with Russia. On April 24, 1945, just one day before the American and Soviet armies linked up on the Elbe, Truman met with Soviet foreign minister Vyacheslav Molotov at the White House. Truman bluntly condemned Soviet actions in Poland and demanded that the Soviet Union live up to the agreements signed at Yalta. Truman later recalled Molotov's stunned response: "I have never been talked to like that in my life," the foreign minister said. "Carry out your agreements," Truman replied, "and you won't get talked to like that."[6]

Potsdam

On May 8, 1945, Germany officially surrendered to the Allied forces, ending World War II in Europe. But while peace had come to Europe, political upheaval continued. The Soviet army had occupied much of Eastern Europe, including East Germany, Bulgaria, Romania, Hungary, Poland, and part of Czechoslovakia. The Baltic States (Estonia, Latvia, and Lithuania) had been absorbed into Russia in 1940. Local Communist governments ruled in Yugoslavia and Albania. In the occupied states, the Soviets supervised "free" elections to ensure that Communist candidates would win. Leaders who acted too independently were forcibly removed from office. The Soviet Union was tightening its grip around Eastern Europe.

In July 1945, another conference of the Big Three nations was held, this time in Potsdam, a suburb of Berlin. Potsdam was the last conference of the war years. Truman, Stalin, and Churchill (who was replaced by the newly elected prime minister Clement Atlee halfway through the conference) met to further discuss how Germany and Japan would be treated after the war. Truman wanted Germany to eventually regain economic stability, while Stalin hoped to seize Germany's industrial wealth as compensation for the losses suffered by the Soviet Union during the war. The president also reprimanded Stalin for his Eastern European policy. "Since the Yalta Conference," Truman read from a prepared statement, "the obligations under this declaration have not been carried out."[7] It was obvious that the postwar goals of the United States and the Soviet Union were still far apart.

With the European war over, the United States could direct its military might to fighting the Pacific war against Japan. While the Potsdam Conference wore on that July, other events were taking place that would have profound implications not only for the war in the Pacific but for the entire postwar world as well. On the day before the Potsdam Conference began, scientists in New Mexico detonated an awesome new weapon that could unleash destructive power unmatched in the history of the world.

The Atomic Age Begins

Daybreak came twice over the New Mexico desert on Monday, July 16, 1945. Just before 5:30 A.M., a brilliant light illuminated the predawn skies over Alamogordo Air Base, a momentary flash that could be seen 250 miles away. The flash was caused by the testing of a new kind of bomb, and the blast it produced rattled windows hundreds of miles from the desert test site. The bomb, nicknamed "Fat Man" for its squat, bulbous shape, was the world's first explosive device based on atomic energy. The explosion triggered on that July morning was equal to seventeen thousand

Truman and Roosevelt

There could hardly be two more different personalities than Franklin D. Roosevelt and the man who succeeded him as president at the outset of the Cold War, Harry S. Truman. In his Pulitzer Prize–winning biography, *Truman*, David McCullough describes the essential differences that shaped the thoughts and actions of these two presidents.

Truman, with his Monday night poker games, his Masonic ring and snappy bow ties, the Main Street pals, the dry Missouri voice, was entirely, undeniably middle American. He had only to open his mouth and his origins were plain. It wasn't just that he came from a particular part of the country, geographically, but from a specific part of the American experience, an authentic pioneer background, and a specific place in the American imagination. His Missouri, as he loved to emphasize, was the Missouri of Mark Twain and Jesse James.

Roosevelt, on the other hand, . . . was the authentic American patrician come to power, no matter that he loved politics or a night of poker with "the boys" quite as much as the senator from Missouri, or that he, too, was a Mason and chose a bow tie as many mornings as not. . . . Roosevelt had been given things all of his life—houses, furniture, servants, travels abroad. Truman had been given almost nothing. He had never had a house to call his own. He had been taught from childhood, and by rough experience, that what he became would depend almost entirely on what he did.

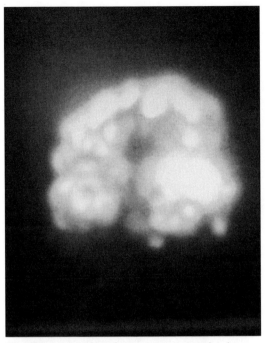

The first atomic bomb test in New Mexico in 1945 marks the birth of the atomic age.

tons of TNT, a destructive power never before released by a single bomb.

The test, code-named Trinity, was the culmination of more than three years of intensive work in numerous installations around the country. Operating under the name Manhattan Engineer District and usually referred to simply as the Manhattan Project, thousands of civilian scientists and military men labored to design and build the atomic bomb in strictest secrecy. Work proceeded day and night, for government officials feared that the Germans were developing their own atomic bomb (America learned after the war that Germany was, in fact, nowhere near produc-

ing a workable atomic device). If successful, the Trinity test would mark the dawn of the atomic age. But as zero hour approached, no one knew for sure if the bomb would even work. Debates among scientists raged over whether Fat Man would be a dud or if it would work too well, possibly destroying New Mexico or even setting fire to the earth's atmosphere. When the test succeeded, the scientists breathed a collective sigh of relief and celebrated their accomplishment. But at least one man realized the terrible implications of such a destructive weapon. After the test, Dr. J. Robert Oppenheimer, chief civilian scientist of the Manhattan Project, recalled a line from a sacred Hindu text: "I am become Death, the shatterer of worlds."[8] If humankind was not careful, the atomic bomb might do just that.

President Harry Truman learned of the success of Trinity on the evening of July 16 via a top-secret cable from Washington. The telegram was written in cryptic medical language to thwart any spies who might try to intercept the message: "Operated on this morning. . . . Diagnosis not yet complete but results seem satisfactory and already exceed expectations."[9] Truman would not receive a full report on the atomic bomb test until July 21. But the knowledge that the United States possessed such a powerful weapon bolstered Truman's confidence during the Potsdam Conference. With the possibility of using the atomic bomb against Japan, Truman no longer had to rely on a Russian alliance to win the Pacific war. He could take a stronger stand with Stalin during the talks and feel less pressure to make concessions to the Soviet leader. David McCullough, a historian and Pulitzer Prize–winning biographer of Harry Truman, sums up the president's reaction to the success of the Manhattan Project:

> Indeed, all three men [Truman, Secretary of War Henry Stimson, and adviser James Byrnes] felt an overwhelming sense of relief—that so much time and effort, that so vast an investment of money and resources had not been futile. It was not just that $2 billion had been spent, but that it was $2 billion that could have been used for the war effort in other ways. The thing worked—it could end the war—and, there was the pride too that a task of such complexity and magnitude, so completely unprecedented, had been an American success.[10]

Truman knew that sooner or later he would have to tell Stalin about the atomic bomb. His opportunity came on July 24, when he approached Stalin after the day's session had ended. He told the Soviet leader only that the United States

Eyewitness to a New Age

Most of the people present at the detonation of the world's first atomic bomb were awestruck by the raw power of the blast. William L. Laurence, a science correspondent for the *New York Times,* was the only reporter at the scene of the Trinity explosion. His dramatic report is included in *The Day the Sun Rose Twice,* a book by Ferenc Morton Szasz.

> The Atomic Age began at exactly 5:30 Mountain War Time on the morning of July 16, 1945, on a stretch of semi-desert land about 50 airline miles from Alamogordo, N.M., just a few minutes before the dawn of a new day on that part of the earth.
>
> Just at that instant, there rose from the bowels of the earth a light not of this world, the light of many suns in one. It was a sunrise such as the world had never seen, a great green super-sun climbing in a fraction of a second to a height of more than 8,000 feet, rising ever higher until it touched the clouds, lighting up earth and sky all around with a dazzling luminosity.
>
> Up it went, a great ball of fire about a mile in diameter, changing colors as it kept shooting upward, from deep purple to orange, expanding, growing bigger, rising as it was expanding, an elemental force freed from its bonds after being chained for billions of years.
>
> For a fleeting instant the color was unearthly green, such as one sees only in the corona of the sun during a total eclipse. It was as though the earth had opened and the skies had split.
>
> One felt as though he had been privileged to witness the Birth of the World—to be present at the moment of Creation when the Lord said: "Let there be light."

Hiroshima is pictured three months after being devastated by the first atomic bomb to be used in warfare.

had a weapon of "unusual destructive force,"[11] but provided no details about the atomic bomb. Stalin's response to the news was puzzling, for he seemed neither surprised nor interested in Truman's revelation. Only much later would the United States learn that Soviet spies had been stealing U.S. nuclear secrets for years.

The Potsdam Conference ended on August 2, 1945. Several agreements were reached, including the handing over of German ships to the Soviet Union as payment for war debts and the setting of a temporary border between Germany and Poland. But the real legacy of Potsdam would lie in the deep-ening distrust between the United States and the Soviet Union. Although Truman later said that he liked Stalin for his straightforward manner, the president nevertheless harbored no illusions about the Soviet premier's ruthless methods of governing his people. "A few top hands," he wrote, "just take clubs, pistols and concentration camps and rule the people on the lowest levels."[12] The rift between democratic and Communist philosophies would widen in the years after World War II.

Stalin's Reign of Terror

Joseph Stalin's rise to power was marked by the elimination of anyone who opposed him. He was responsible for the deaths of millions of people in the years before World War II. In his book *The Rise and Fall of Stalin,* author Robert Payne describes Stalin's ruthless methods, giving an insight into the backdrop of fear with which people in Communist Russia lived.

By 1937 Stalin had reached the stage when murder had become as habitual as shaving or eating. Three or four times a week the death lists compiled by [head of the secret police Nikolai] Yezhov at his orders would be presented to him, he would read through the lists casually, add his initials, and then forget about them. These lists did not comprise the names of a small number of high officials, but included hundreds and sometimes thousands of obscure people working inside and outside the government. In many cases the lists were mere formalities: the people had already been shot. These drab pages filled with names represented the only currency he recognized: they were his bills of trading in the endless terror he was visiting upon Russia. ... To the end of his life Stalin continued to initial three or four death lists weekly. He felt neither pleasure nor pain; only a profound indifference. His soul was burdened with so many crimes that he had long ago forgotten that it was possible to live without committing them. Murder was the air he breathed, his sole justification, the key that turned all the locks.

Joseph Stalin ruthlessly murdered thousands of Soviet citizens.

The End of the War

Truman was aboard the USS *Augusta* on August 6, 1945, sailing home from Potsdam, when, at his direction, an atomic bomb was dropped on the Japanese city of Hiroshima. Some eighty thousand people died instantly, and thousands more would later perish from injuries and radiation sickness. Although demands for surrender had been sent to the Japanese, only silence emanated from the emperor's palace in Tokyo. Three days later, on August 9, another atomic bomb was dropped, this time on the city of Nagasaki. The bomb, nicknamed "Fat Man" like the one detonated at Trinity, killed an estimated seventy thousand people. Within twenty-four hours, Japanese emperor Hirohito came to the realization that his nation could not resist and survive. On September 2, 1945, the deck of the battleship USS *Missouri* was the scene of the official Japanese surrender. After the Japanese foreign minister and army chief of staff signed the surrender document, General Douglas MacArthur did the same for the Allied forces. Then MacArthur said, "Let us pray that peace be now restored to the world and that God will preserve it always."[13] But the peace that followed would be an uneasy one.

After three and a half years of war, Americans wanted nothing more than to return to their normal, peaceful way of life. The first step in this process was to demobilize the American armed forces. President Truman, a veteran of World War I, realized that keeping the military strong was important even in times of peace. If another conflict that involved American interests should arise, a peacetime army or navy could be mobilized quickly to confront potential enemies. Truman even suggested to Congress that mandatory military training be established to provide such a ready armed force. But America's longing for peace was too strong for even the president to resist. From the end of the war in 1945, U.S. military strength fell from 12 million soldiers, sailors, and airmen to 1.5 million by June 1947. The Soviet Union also reduced its armed forces after the war, decreasing its military by nearly 75 percent. But even with these cutbacks, in 1948 the Soviet military was twice as large as the U.S. armed forces with some

3 million soldiers. And that number would increase to 5 million over the next five years.

A Changing Europe

After the war, Soviet premier Joseph Stalin and his Red Army were considered heroes in the minds of much of the American public. The valiant way in which Russian soldiers fought against the Germans, as well as the staggering loss of some 20 million Russian soldiers and civilians during the war, tended to overshadow the atrocities committed by Stalin's regime in the 1930s. The Soviet Union was seen as a nation longing to be friends with the United States, led by a head of state who had been given the disarming nickname "Uncle Joe." Even General Dwight D. Eisenhower, the supreme commander of the Allied forces in Europe, declared that "nothing guides Russian policy so much as a desire for friendship with the United States."[14] The truth, however, was much more sinister than Americans knew.

In addition to the Soviet occupation of Eastern European countries, Russian troops were also stationed in parts of Manchuria and Iran. The Communist Party had become the largest political party in both France and Italy, making it a formidable political force in Central Europe. And Stalin had strong opinions about the American president who had replaced Roosevelt. Although Truman had confessed to liking if not really trusting the

Soviet premier, Stalin had secretly called Truman "worthless."

On February 9, 1946, Stalin publicly affirmed his contempt for the American way of life in a speech given to Soviet voters at the Grand Opera House in Moscow. According to Stalin, history had shown that capitalism and communism were incompatible and that the Soviet way of life was the superior way. World War II, Stalin said, "broke out as an inevitable result of the development of world economic and political forces on the basis of modern monopoly capitalism. Marxists have stated more than once that the capitalist system of world economy conceals in itself the elements of general crisis and military clashes. . . . The

Soviet social system is a better form of organization of society than any non-Soviet social system."[15] Stalin further called for increased industrial and military production to prepare the Soviet Union for any future eventualities, perhaps including an armed confrontation between the two ideologies.

The Long Telegram

In February 1946, just two weeks after Stalin delivered his preelection speech in Moscow, a telegram arrived at the State Department in Washington. The cable, bearing the innocuous designation of Dispatch No. 511, was no routine government message. It was so long that it was sent in five parts, and its point of origin

The Iron Curtain

Only nine months after the end of WWII, at Westminster College in the small town of Fulton, Missouri, former British prime minister Winston Churchill gave a speech on U.S.-Soviet relations that to many historians marks the beginning of the Cold War. On the evening of March 5, 1946, President Truman introduced Churchill to a crowd waiting for the Westminster commencement exercises to begin. Churchill remarked on his admiration for the Russian people. Then, as quoted in *Truman* by David McCullough, he dramatically warned that the Soviets were extending their influence in violation of the Yalta agreements:

> From Stettin in the Baltic to Trieste in the Adriatic, an iron curtain had descended across the Continent. Behind that line lie all the capitals of the ancient states of Central and Eastern Europe. Warsaw, Berlin, Prague,

Vienna, Budapest, Belgrade, Bucharest and Sofia, all these famous cities and the populations around them lie in what I must call the Soviet sphere, and all are subject in one form or another, not only to Soviet influence but to a very high and, in many cases, increasing measure of control from Moscow.

Churchill did not invent the phrase "iron curtain," but with his speech the words popularly and permanently described the postwar split between East and West. The speech immediately provoked a flurry of criticism that Churchill was calling for armed conflict with the Soviet Union. Stalin himself labeled the speech a virtual declaration of war. Truman, who had invited Churchill to come to Missouri and had enthusiastically approved of his remarks, had to reverse his endorsement in the face of increasing public disapproval.

George Kennan (far right) authored the "Long Telegram," which detailed his pessimistic view of Soviet-American relations.

was the American embassy in Moscow. The information it contained would set the tone for the Cold War.

The author of the eight-thousand-word dispatch was George F. Kennan, the chargé d'affaires, or temporary head, of the embassy. In his message, which became known as the "Long Telegram," Kennan's pessimistic view of Soviet-American relations came through loud and clear. He warned that the Soviet Union would continue to expand its domination of non-Communist countries, and at the same time act to reduce the international influence of capitalism. Plagued by a traditional Russian sense of insecurity, the Soviets would take every opportunity to exploit the differences between the various capitalist powers in an effort to weaken them. Kennan urged the United States to realize that peaceful co-existence with Russia was not possible; the Soviet Union, he said flatly, was an adversary that had to be dealt with. In fact, he concluded, coping with the Soviet threat would be the "greatest task our diplomacy has ever faced and probably the greatest it will ever have to face."[16]

Kennan's telegram would have a long-term impact in Washington on the nature of Soviet-American relations. Secretary of the Navy James Forrestal was so impressed that he had hundreds of copies circulated throughout the highest levels of government. Truman read the telegram but did not take any immediate action on the information it contained. The Long Telegram, however, would remain one of the Cold War's earliest and most important documents.

Less than a year after the end of World War II, most Americans were unaware of or indifferent to the reality of Soviet aggression in Eastern Europe. The most devastating war in history had just ended, and living in a new world of peace was uppermost in everyone's mind. But the reality of this new world included forces that ordinary citizens could neither control nor fully understand. Another war was on the horizon, a war not of guns and tanks and marching soldiers but of ideologies and politics and fear. And for the United States there was a new opponent. The Soviet Union, America's World War II ally, had become its postwar adversary.

Chapter 2

The Cold War Begins

In July 1946 President Harry Truman commissioned his special counsel Clark Clifford to prepare a report on the state of U.S.-Soviet relations. "American Relations with the Soviet Union," completed in September 1946, was nearly 100,000 words long and contained an alarming account of the growth of Russia's political and military power. The Soviet Union, the report stated, opposed U.S. efforts at establishing world peace so that Red Army troops could remain in occupied countries. Stalin was further extending his political hold not only in Europe but in the Middle East, China, Korea, and Southeast Asia as well. Most ominous, the Soviet military was gaining strength, with emphasis on the development of atomic weapons, submarines, missiles, and biological warfare agents.

Truman was already familiar with most of the facts contained in Clifford's report, some of which had appeared in George Kennan's Long Telegram. But the likely impact of so much information consolidated into one document troubled the president. He immediately ordered all copies to be locked away, afraid that any leak would have disastrous consequences on his efforts to achieve peace in the world. George Elsey, Clifford's assistant who did much of the research and writing of "American Relations with the Soviet Union," later summarized the report:

> The point was, we had to recognize the Soviets were on an expansionist binge, if you will. They were going to extend their sphere of influence as far as they possibly could. And at any point where they sensed weakness on the part of the United States and Western Europe, they would press forward. And it would not only be in Western Europe, it would be in the Middle East and, to the extent they

could, it would be in Southeast Asia, India, as well.[17]

The problem with the Soviet Union had now been defined and it was time for the United States to come up with a solution. The burden of determining that solution rested squarely on the shoulders of President Harry Truman.

Trouble in Greece

In 1947 the region of the Mediterranean Sea became the focal point for the creation of U.S. policy toward Soviet expansionism. For weeks in early 1947, Truman had been receiving warnings about the stability of the Mediterranean nation of Greece. Since Greece had been liberated from German occupation in 1944, the conservative government repeatedly clashed with Communist insurgents in a struggle for control of the country. The only thing keeping the Communists in check was the British backing, in the form of troops and financial aid, received by the Greek government. If that aid were removed, Greece would surely become a Communist state.

On February 21, 1947, an urgent diplomatic note, or "blue paper," from the British ambassador was delivered to the U.S. State Department. It carried bad news: Great Britain, its economy devastated by World War II, could no longer afford to

Greek commandos are pictured in their fight against Communist insurgents.

support the conservative Greek government. By March 31, Britain would withdraw its troops from Greece and end all financial aid. The ambassador hoped that the United States could take up the burden of defending the beleaguered nation.

Greece was not the only Mediterranean nation at risk. Turkey was being pressured by the Soviet Union to share control of the Dardanelles, the straits connecting the Mediterranean and the landlocked Black Sea. Clearly, the Mediterranean region was becoming a powder keg that, if ignited, could have dire consequences for the United States. General George C. Marshall, the army's chief of staff during World War II and now Truman's secretary of state, commented, "It is not alarmist to say that we are faced with the first crisis of a series which might extend Soviet domination to Europe, the Middle East and Asia."[18]

A British soldier is wounded in the Greek Communist rebellion in 1948.

The Truman Doctrine

At just after 1:00 P.M. on March 12, 1947, President Truman addressed a joint session of Congress and a radio audience of concerned Americans. In the hushed atmosphere of the House Chamber, a dark-suited Truman spoke of two alternative ways of life: one based on the free will of the people and the other based on political repression. Then he declared that the United States had a responsibility to help other countries resist the growing tide of oppression. "I believe," Truman said, "that it must be the policy of the United

States to support free peoples who are resisting attempted subjugation by armed minorities or by outside pressures."[19] Although he did not mention the Soviet Union by name, his implication of the Communist regime was clear.

Truman asked Congress for $400 million in aid for Greece and Turkey. Without such help, he said, the consequences would be far reaching to both the West and the East. The president solemnly concluded his speech with the assertion that the situation in the Mediterranean was serious: "I would not recommend [this course of action] except that the alternative is much more serious. . . . If we falter in our leadership, we may endanger the peace of the world, and we shall surely endanger the welfare of this nation."[20] Despite congressional worries that Truman's sweeping statement of support for "free peoples" would entangle the United States in all sorts of international disputes, the House approved Truman's plan on April 22, 1947, and on May 9 the Senate did likewise. On May 22 President Truman affixed his signature to the document providing $400 million in aid to Greece and Turkey.

The principle that the United States had a responsibility to help oppressed nations became known as the Truman Doctrine. It was an important turning point in the early years of the Cold War for it established that, from now on, the United States would respond to Communist threats abroad. The specifics of just how it would respond still had to be defined. One man who had a plan was Secretary of State George Marshall.

The Marshall Plan

Economic problems were by no means confined to the island nation of Great Britain. The lingering consequences of World War II were causing hardships all across the continent as well. Although the war had been over for two years, the European economy had not recovered. European countries had too little cash to spend or invest and too few goods to sell.

Food was scarce, and there was a drastic shortage of coal, steel, oil, and other essential raw materials. In addition, the bitterly cold winter of 1946–1947 was one of the worst in recent memory, further adding to the suffering of people whose homelands had already been devastated by six years of war. The precarious economic state of postwar Europe had implications for the United States, as well. The loss of European markets for American goods could spell disaster for the U.S. economy, and in the collapse of any of these countries lurked the danger of Communist intervention.

On recent visits to Paris and Berlin, George Marshall had seen firsthand the conditions that Europe endured. Upon his return to the United States, he assembled a panel to devise a solution to the European problem. Speaking at the Harvard University commencement exercises on June 5, 1947, Marshall announced a plan for the economic revival of Europe. Marshall's program called for European nations to get together and determine what they needed to rebuild their economies and then submit these needs to the United States for review and, ultimately, funding. This generous offer was open to all European countries, including the Soviet Union and its satellite nations. "Our policy," Marshall said in his speech, "is directed not against any country or doctrine, but against hunger, poverty, desperation and chaos. Its purpose should be the revival of a working economy in the world so as to permit the emergence of political and social conditions in which free institutions can exist."[21]

Officially called the European Recovery Program, it was more popularly known as the Marshall Plan after its able administrator (Truman suggested the designation, fearing that the Republican Congress would reject any plan that bore his own name). Operating from 1948 to 1952, the Marshall Plan became a major factor in the postwar recovery of Europe, distributing some $13 billion to sixteen European nations, primarily for rebuilding power plants and revitalizing the iron and steel industries. None of those nations, however, was in the Soviet-dominated Eastern European bloc. Afraid that Western aid would weaken its grip on the satellite countries it controlled, the Soviet Union refused to participate in the Marshall Plan. After attending a meeting in Paris to discuss the Marshall Plan, Soviet foreign minister Vyacheslav Molotov reported his impressions to Stalin. "Under the guise of formulating a plan for the reconstruction of Europe," Molotov said, the United States was seeking to "interfere in the internal affairs of European countries, impose an American program upon them, and ban them from selling their surpluses where they choose

Two Berlin residents confer in front of a poster supporting the Marshall Plan.

to, thus making the economies of these countries dependent on U.S. interests."[22]

Viewing the Marshall Plan as yet another threat by the Western powers, the Soviet Union missed an opportunity to rebuild Eastern Europe, thus dooming the region to remain economically weak. As the economic split between Western and Eastern European nations developed, the Soviet Union began to tighten its political grip on the Eastern bloc. The United States, in turn, would have to come up with some way to oppose the spread of communism.

Containing Communism

In July 1947, an article in the influential magazine *Foreign Affairs* created a stir in Washington. Titled "The Sources of Soviet Conduct," it was written by a mysterious author identified only as "X." The article discussed U.S.-Soviet relations and ways in which the United States could effectively deal with its former ally. But within the article was one word that would give a name to the principle behind the Truman Doctrine and the Marshall Plan: *containment.* "In these circumstances," the anonymous author wrote, "it is clear that the main element of any United States policy toward the Soviet Union must be that of long-term, patient but firm and vigilant containment of Russian expansive tendencies."[23]

The press immediately latched onto the word *containment* as a concise description of American foreign policy regarding the Soviet Union. Before long, the word was being repeated not only by official Washington but also by ordinary citizens, thanks to portions of the article reprinted in such popular magazines as *Life* and *Reader's Digest.*

It was soon revealed that the anonymous author "X" was none other than George F. Kennan, who had written the Long Telegram the year before. Kennan later said that the importance of his article was exaggerated and that he meant containment in a political, not military, sense. Nevertheless, the term *containment* became part of the popular language. There was now an official cause to rally around, and everyone knew that they must contain Communist expansion or suffer dire, as-yet unknown, consequences.

Crisis in Berlin

With Marshall Plan aid on its way, Soviet dictator Joseph Stalin was in a difficult position. If the plan succeeded, he could no longer count on a weakened Western Europe ripe for a Communist takeover. Thus, Stalin would have to concentrate on solidifying his power in Eastern Europe. In February 1948 a Soviet-backed coup overthrew the democratic government of Czechoslovakia, the last independent country behind the Iron Curtain. But of even more concern to Stalin was the nation that had invaded Russia in World War II: Germany.

The Yalta Conference in 1945 had decreed that Germany be divided into four occupation zones. The western part of the nation held three of those zones, administered by American, British, and French armies of occupation. Germany's eastern region was occupied by Stalin's Red Army. Representatives of the four occupying nations formed the Allied Control Council to jointly oversee the four zones. Berlin, Germany's capital before 1945, was also divided into four sectors, and its occupation was similar to that of the nation. The Soviet Union controlled the eastern sector, while the British, French, and Americans supervised the west. But this divided city lay deep within

Dealing with the Russians

In his assignment as the head of the U.S. embassy in Moscow, George F. Kennan got to know the Russian mind perhaps better than most Westerners at that time. Even before he wrote his famous Long Telegram, Kennan penned a document called "The United States and Russia," a plan for dealing with Communists, specifically the Communists of the Stalin regime. Although never officially used, the document, excerpted below from Kennan's *Memoirs, 1925–1950*, gives a fascinating insight into the obstacles inherent in trying to negotiate with a culture very different from one's own.

The Russians, throughout their history, have dealt principally with fierce hostile neighbors. Lacking natural geographic barriers, they have had to develop, in order to deal with these neighbors, a particular technique (now become traditional and almost automatic) of elastic advance and retreat, of defense in depth, of secretiveness, of wariness, of deceit. Their history has known many armistices between hostile forces; but it has never known an example of the permanent peaceful coexistence of two neighboring states with established borders accepted without question by both peoples. The Russians therefore have no conception of permanent friendly relations between states. For them, all foreigners are potential enemies. The technique of Russian diplomacy. . . is concentrated on impressing an adversary with the terrifying strength of Russian power, while keeping him uncertain and confused as to the exact channels and means of its application and thus inducing him to treat all Russian wishes and views with particular respect and consideration. It has nothing to do with the cultivation of friendly relations as we conceive them.

We would find it much easier to deal with Russia if we would recognize frankly in our own minds the fact that its leaders are, by their own choice, the enemies of all that part of the world they do not control, and that this is a recognized principle of thought and action for the entire Soviet machine.

Soviet-controlled territory, a small island surrounded by Communist influence.

By 1946, the United States felt it was time to begin rebuilding Germany. Although no one wanted to see Germany become a formidable military power again, its economic recovery was necessary for the development of a strong postwar Europe. In December 1946 the United States and Great Britain agreed to consolidate their zones in western Germany, forming a "Bizone" that would take effect on January 1, 1947. In response to this strengthening of democratic western Germany, the Soviet Union withdrew its delegate from the Allied Control Council. The separation of Germany into two opposing parts had begun.

On June 18, 1948, the United States and Britain announced that a new form of currency would begin circulating in West Germany. This new money—the deutschmark—had a profound effect on Soviet plans for Germany. The Soviets had promoted inflation, or high prices combined with low currency value, in the country in order to keep Germany economically weak and therefore dependent on the Soviet Union. The introduction of the deutschmark would mean a stronger West Germany with closer ties to the West. Soviet retaliation came swiftly.

On the same night that the announcement of the new currency was being broadcast by radio across Germany, Soviet military authorities began halting automo-

The Allied commanders of the occupation forces in Germany's four zones stand at attention in 1945.

bile, rail, and pedestrian traffic from West Germany to Berlin. "Technical difficulties" was the official Soviet explanation, which nobody in the West believed. By June 24 all travel by road, rail, or water into and out of Berlin ceased. All over the city, lights began to flicker and then go out as electric power was cut off. With Berlin's lifelines to the West severed, food, coal, and other vital materials could no longer be brought to the 2.5 million people who lived in the besieged city. The Soviets were determined to force Berlin to join their side by starving it into submission.

The Berlin Blockade was the first major crisis of the Cold War and could have led to World War III if the United States mishandled its response to the Soviet Union's actions. Truman stood firm in his resolve to support the citizens of West Berlin. When it was suggested that the United States pull its troops out of Berlin, Truman's answer was short and to the point: "We stay in Berlin, period."[24] With all ground routes blockaded, the United States looked to the sky as an avenue for relief.

On June 28, 1948, "Operation Vittles," the Berlin Airlift's unofficial name, began ferrying supplies into Berlin. Airpower, which had proved so vital to the Allied victory in World War II, now proved equally effective in bringing relief to Berlin. U.S. and British pilots flew night and day, in good weather and bad, to keep the supply lines flowing. Aircraft delivered four thousand tons a day of food, medicine, fuel, salt, and other ne-

cessities to two Berlin airports, Gatow and Templehof. The drone of aircraft engines constantly filled the air. At the height of the airlift, planes landed or took off every ninety seconds.

The citizens of Berlin were grateful to the daring pilots who risked their lives to come to their aid (there were seventy-nine military and civilian casualties during the Berlin Airlift). They knitted sweaters and scarves for the pilots and offered precious personal possessions as gifts. Even the youngest Berliners showed their appreciation. "As long as I live," says Stuart Symington, former secretary of the air force, "I'll never forget the little German children who'd come out to the airport with flowers . . . , and greet us when we got out of plane."[25]

By early 1949, the Soviet Union realized that its blockade of Berlin was doomed to failure. Flights continued to bring relief to Berlin unhindered by the Soviets. In all, throughout the eleven months of the blockade, more than 270,000 flights delivered over 2.3 million tons of goods to Berlin. The airlift pilots were regarded by the world as heroes, while the Soviets were seen as brutes trying to starve innocent people. After a series of private negotiations, on May 12, 1949, the Soviet Union lifted the Berlin Blockade. Soon, trucks were once again rumbling across the Berlin border, carrying the supplies that, for nearly a year, had reached Berlin only by air.

The Chocolate Flier

The Berlin Blockade affected everyone in the city, children as well as adults. In this excerpt from their book *The Berlin Airlift,* British journalists Ann and John Tusa tell the story of a special pilot who came up with an idea to make the blockade a little less difficult for the children of Berlin.

One day in autumn 1948 a twenty-seven-year-old pilot from Utah, Gail Halvorsen, wandered off the station at Templehof and met some children. He stopped for a pidgin and mime chat. They were nice, cheerful children, but there was something odd about them which puzzled Halvorsen. Then it struck him: every other child the world over asked for chocolate or gum, but these little Berliners did not seem to imagine such a treat. This, thought Halvorsen, was wrong. He told them to wait that evening at the end of the runway, look up and see what happened. Back at base he went to work with some handkerchiefs. Next time he was about to touch down at Templehof he gave a signal to his crew chief and a sprinkling of candy parachuted to the ground. He could hardly stop there: the children would be waiting. So every trip the "Sweet Bomber," the *"Schokoladen Flieger"* [Chocolate Flier], did another parachute drop. He soon ran out of hankies and old shirts; friends joined in with cloth and cargo. News spread; chocolate, sweets and gum appeared from other bases and the United States. By October Halvorsen had a staff of six to deal with the supplies and thank-you letters, the German Youth Activities group was engaged in mass production of parachutes, and the USAF was running "Operation Little Vittles," dropping 6,000 consignments of goodies a day.

Children eagerly await the landing of a U.S. cargo plane during the Berlin Airlift.

The Berlin Airlift was one of America's greatest Cold War achievements. It showed the world that the United States had the technology—and the courage—to stand up to the Soviet Union. But in its wake a divided Berlin stood as a symbol of the ideological split between East and West.

A European Alliance

Although the Soviet Union had finally backed down in the face of the successful Berlin Airlift, it was still a formidable presence in Europe—especially in terms of military strength. Twenty divisions of the Red Army, mostly situated in East Germany, remained a shadow hovering over Eastern Europe. The nations of Western Europe, although recovering economically thanks to the Marshall Plan, still worried about Soviet military aggression. If the Soviets could blockade Berlin, who knew what they might try next?

Following a series of meetings that had begun in early 1948, the United States, Canada, and ten European nations formed the North Atlantic Treaty Organization (NATO) on April 4, 1949. The purpose of NATO was to bind together the member nations in an agreement of mutual cooperation and protection. According to the treaty, an attack by an armed aggressor against any one NATO nation would be considered an attack on all of the members. At the signing ceremony, which was broadcast live over radio and the new medium of television, President Truman said that the treaty "would create a shield against aggression and fear of aggression—a bulwark

President Truman signs the treaty establishing the North Atlantic Treaty Organization.

The Nations of NATO

The North Atlantic Treaty Organization is one of the most important alliances to come into existence after World War II. For President Harry S. Truman, it was tangible evidence of his commitment to prevent future world wars. Excerpts of his remarks made at the signing ceremony, including the one below, can be found in *The Origins of NATO: The North Atlantic Treaty Organization* at the Department of State website.

> For us, war is not inevitable. We do not believe that there are blind tides of history which sweep men one way or the other. In our own time we have seen brave men overcome obstacles that seemed insurmountable and forces that seemed over-

whelming. Men with courage and vision can still determine their own destiny. They can choose slavery or freedom—war or peace. I have no doubt which they will choose. The treaty we are signing here today is evidence of the path they will follow. If there's anything inevitable in the future, it is the will of the people of the world from freedom and peace.

Twelve nations were founding members of NATO: the United States, Canada, the United Kingdom, France, Italy, Portugal, the Netherlands, Norway, Denmark, Iceland, Belgium, and Luxembourg. Since then, seven more nations—Germany, Spain, Greece, Hungary, Turkey, Poland, and the Czech Republic—have joined.

which will permit us to get on with the real business of government and society, the business of achieving a fuller and happier life for all our citizens."[26]

Membership in NATO was, for the United States, a major shift in foreign policy. It marked the first time in history that the United States became part of a military alliance in peacetime. In number, the U.S. armed forces were still no match for the Soviet troops in Eastern Europe, and in 1955 the Soviet Union would strengthen its grip by forming its own alliance, the Warsaw Pact. But America's commitment to European unity was clear. Besides, the United States had the advantage of being the only nation with atomic weapons. That situation, however, was about to change, altering the entire face of the Cold War.

A New Superpower

On September 3, 1949, a sleek, silver B-29 aircraft, the type of plane used to drop the atomic bombs on Japan, soared high above the northern Pacific Ocean, flying between Japan and Alaska. The plane was on a routine weather reconnaissance patrol, and it carried not bombs but sensitive equipment for sampling the air at high altitudes. One sample taken that day showed a peculiar rise in the level of radioactivity in the atmosphere. Additional samples confirmed the abnormal reading. After studying the test data for several days, a group of scientists came to a disturbing conclusion: Somewhere in Siberia, the Soviet Union had detonated an atomic bomb.

The news caught Washington unprepared. Although many atomic scientists had predicted that the Soviet Union would be able to produce an atomic bomb within five years after the end of World War II, others were skeptical. General Leslie Groves, the military head of America's atomic bomb program, the Manhattan Project, predicted it would take the Soviets ten to twenty years. President Truman thought they would never produce an atomic bomb. Secretary Symington recalls his own reaction to the news:

> I'll never forget the morning that General [Lauris] Norstad came in and said to me, "I have bad news for you. The Soviets have just exploded an atomic weapon." And I said, "Laurie, that can't be true. It's impossible. They couldn't have done it based on what everybody says." And he said, "Well, they've done it."[27]

The Soviet Union had indeed "done it." In the blink of an eye, America no longer held a monopoly on atomic weapons, and the world was now a different and more dangerous place. On September 23, President Truman released a statement informing the American people that the United States had evidence of an atomic explosion in the Soviet Union. While the public pondered the meaning of this information, Truman was working behind the scenes to cope with the threat it implied. He called on the National Security Council (an advisory agency con-

A cutaway model of the Soviet version of the atomic bomb.

cerned with matters of national security) to review America's role in the new world created by the Soviet bomb. The council's report, designated NSC-68, was given to the president in April 1950. The report warned that, without military might to back it up, the U.S. policy of containment was little more than a bluff. America's armed forces were woefully inadequate for the task, it continued, including the arsenal of atomic weapons, which could be equaled by the Soviet Union by 1954. NSC-68 concluded by urging Americans to take the Cold War seriously: "The whole success hangs ultimately on recognition by this government, the American people and all the peoples that the Cold War is in fact a real war in which the survival of the world is at stake."[28]

Truman read the National Security Council's report but took no immediate action. Torn between the report's recommendation to build up the armed forces and the enormous costs of doing so, the president wondered whether the benefits of rearmament outweighed the expense. But while Truman hesitated, events thousands of miles from the United States would ultimately make the decision for him. For in the small Asian nation of Korea, the Cold War was about to heat up.

<star> **Chapter 3** <star>

Cold War Battlefronts

The Cold War soon became a multifaceted, global conflict. In the United States people were accused of being Communists without a shred of evidence against them. Soviet and American spies alike went to extreme lengths in far-flung places to steal enemy secrets. And communism gained momentum as it established footholds in the Far East, an area of the world Americans regarded as mysterious and unfathomable. In October 1949, after a three-year civil war, the huge nation of China fell to the Communists under the leadership of Mao Tse-tung, driving the Nationalist government to the island of Formosa (now Taiwan).

The nation of Korea juts out into the Sea of Japan, bordered on the west by China, by Russia at its northeast corner, and with mainland Japan a mere one hundred miles off its southeastern coast. This ancient peninsula, located some seven thousand miles from the United States,

would become a flash point in the struggle between communism and democracy as the Cold War escalated at midcentury. With the Cold War heating up, not only Americans but the entire world began to take notice of the ideological struggle that would come to dominate life in the 1950s and beyond.

A Nation Divided

For centuries, the land now known as Korea was called Choson, the "land of the morning calm." In 1910 that calm was shattered when Japan seized and annexed its neighbor to the west, making Korea a Japanese colony. Japan imposed a brutal rule on the Korean people, confiscating farmland and crushing dissent. During World War II, thousands of Koreans were forced to labor for the Japanese war effort or were drafted into the Imperial Japanese Army. As early as 1943, Allied leaders had discussed the fate of a postwar Korea once Japan had been defeated. At the

Yalta Conference in 1945, President Franklin D. Roosevelt proposed that the United States, China, and the Soviet Union jointly oversee the transformation of Korea from a Japanese subject to an independent nation.

On August 10, 1945, the day Japanese emperor Hirohito announced that his country would surrender, Soviet troops invaded Manchuria, a Japanese-held province of China just north of Korea. After defeating the Japanese occupation troops, the Red Army pushed south across the border into northern Korea. This Soviet invasion caused concern in Washington. With the nearest American forces nearly seven hundred miles away on the island of Okinawa, what was to stop the Soviet army from simply overrunning the entire country? At the same time, Japan's capitulation meant that arrangements for the surrender of Japanese soldiers in Korea had to be made. U.S. officials would have to work fast to come up with a solution.

At a late-night meeting in Washington, military officers and diplomats decided that an imaginary line would be drawn across Korea at the 38th parallel, approximately in the middle of the peninsula. North of that line, Japanese soldiers would surrender to the Soviets; once they arrived in Korea,

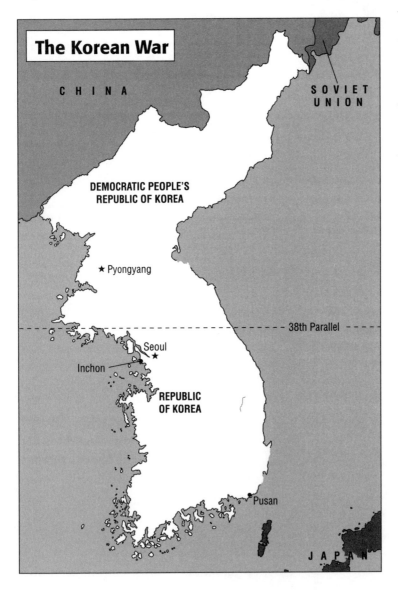

The Korean War

CHINA

SOVIET UNION

DEMOCRATIC PEOPLE'S REPUBLIC OF KOREA

★ Pyongyang

- - - - 38th Parallel - - - -

Seoul ★
Inchon

REPUBLIC OF KOREA

Pusan

JAPAN

American forces would accept the surrenders south of the line. The location of the line itself had no geographical or cultural significance; it was chosen mainly because it already appeared on maps of Korea. It was intended to be temporary, simply a convenient way to facilitate the Japanese surrender. But by 1948 the 38th parallel had become a permanent rift, splitting Korea into two opposing camps. In the south, the Republic of Korea (ROK), under seventy-three-year-old President Syngman Rhee, was a democracy supported by the United States. The Democratic People's Republic of Korea (DPRK, or North Korea) was a Communist government, headed by Premier Kim Il-sung and backed by the Soviet Union.

Soon, both the United States and the Soviet Union began pulling troops out of Korea, and by 1950 only a few advisers remained in both the north and the south. When the U.S. combat troops were gone, Premier Kim (with the approval of Stalin) set in motion a plan to unite Korea under Communist rule.

Invasion

On June 25, 1950, some ninety thousand North Korean troops armed with Soviet weapons and supported by 150 Russian-made T-34 tanks crossed the 38th parallel and invaded South Korea. Caught by surprise, the overwhelmed South Korean army was pushed back toward Seoul, the Republic of Korea's capital. Three days later, Seoul fell to the invading army.

President Truman learned of the invasion of South Korea by a telephone call to his Missouri home from Secretary of State Dean Acheson. Truman immediately realized the seriousness of the situation. Aboard his airplane *Independence* on the flight back to Washington, the president considered how this invasion could escalate into a far more serious conflict and decided that the United States had to act. He later wrote down his thoughts about this troubling time:

> I remembered how each time that the democracies failed to act it encouraged the aggressors to keep going ahead. . . . If the Communists were permitted to force their way into the Republic of Korea without opposition from the free world, no small nation would have the courage to resist threats and aggression by stronger Communist neighbors. If this was allowed to go unchallenged, it would mean a third world war, just as similar incidents had brought on the second world war.[29]

Historians have long debated the reasons for America's entry into the Korean War. Truman and others in Washington saw military intervention as a way of preventing the spread of communism in Asia and, perhaps, the rest of the world. "At the time," writes Korean veteran and military correspondent Harry Summers, "it was assumed that 'monolithic world communism,' controlled and directed by Soviet Premier Joseph Stalin in Moscow, was spreading by force of arms and that Korea was merely the first step in a Communist plan for world conquest."[30] But Communist leaders may have seen the Korean conflict as merely a civil war between two parts of a divided nation, providing a chance to help that nation turn Communist. Kim Il-sung, along with his Soviet sponsors, thought the North Korean army could quickly conquer the south and doubted that the United States would intervene with military force. They soon realized that they were mistaken.

Desperate South Korean refugees flee North Korean troops.

The United Nations Responds

Upon receiving the news of the invasion of South Korea, President Truman called on the United Nations to condemn the attack and to resolve that UN member nations would come to the aid of the Republic of Korea. Established at the end of World War II to resolve international disputes and promote world peace, the United Nations was now faced with its first real crisis. The UN Security Council, a group of eleven major powers and smaller countries, resolved to send UN troops to South Korea. As a member of the Security Council, the Soviet Union could have vetoed this resolution. But its representative was boycotting the United Nations over a controversy concerning the seating of Communist China in the council. The Soviet representative soon returned to the council, but it was too late. On July 24, 1950, the resolution was passed forming the United Nations Command. For the first time in history, an international organization would join the fight against communism, with fifteen member nations eventually entering the hostilities in Korea.

Even before the UN resolution was passed, President Truman authorized the use of U.S. air and naval forces in Korea, acting under presidential authority rather than a formal declaration of war. Indeed, the Korean conflict would often be referred to as a "police action" rather than a war.

At first, the American troops fared no better than the South Korean soldiers against the North Korean army. By August, the U.S. and ROK forces had been pushed back to the southern tip of Korea, establishing a defensive perimeter around the city of Pusan. On September 15 General Douglas MacArthur, commander in chief of the United Nations Command, staged a daring amphibious invasion of the Korean port city of Inchon. This bold stroke some 150 miles inside Communist-held territory prevented a swift victory for the North Korean army. Soon, U.S. troops had recaptured Seoul.

China Enters the War

The Inchon invasion completely changed the face of the Korean War. Within days, the North Korean army was in full retreat. By October 1950, the Communist forces had been pushed back north of the 38th parallel; the main objective of the UN resolution had been achieved. But President Truman decided that, rather than stopping at the 38th parallel, it would be in the best interests of the United States and the world if communism in Korea were "rolled back." The risk inherent in such a move was that it might bring Communist Chinese or Soviet troops into the war and trigger a wider conflict, possibly even World War III. MacArthur had assured Truman that he saw little chance of that happening. Truman agreed, and on October 9 UN forces moved into North Korea.

MacArthur's troops pushed the North Korean army toward the Yalu River, the border between North Korea and China. On the other side of the river, however, there were ominous signs of a massive Chinese Communist military buildup. MacArthur dismissed the reports. Han Xu, China's ambassador to the United States, later wrote, "We repeatedly gave warning to the United States not to cross the 38th parallel and not to approach our border. . . . But it was simply written off as a Communist bluff and all

propaganda and ignored. It turned out it was not a bluff."[31]

In an attempt to end the war by Christmas of 1950, General MacArthur launched a major offensive on November 24, the day after Thanksgiving. To nearly everyone's surprise, the assault was met by more than a quarter-million Chinese Communist troops who had already crossed the Yalu River into

Members of the United Nations debate a proposal to send UN troops to South Korea.

Combat in Korea

Just five years after World War II ended, the United States became involved in another armed conflict, the first "hot" flareup of the Cold War years. Just as names like Normandy, Iwo Jima, and the Battle of the Bulge have become enduring symbols of World War II, so, too, did Korea have its symbols: Inchon, the Pusan Perimeter, and Porkchop Hill. The book *No Bugles, No Drums* by Rudy Tomedi presents a history of the Korean War in the words of those who fought there. In the following excerpt, Sherman Pratt, a World War II veteran who also fought in Korea, gives a glimpse of combat over a piece of territory known as Heartbreak Ridge.

> I can fully understand how that place got its name, because it was just heartbreaking to watch. I could see the mortar rounds and artillery exploding among the men as they were trying to fight their way up these steep ridges. Even without binoculars I could see them scrambling around on the slopes, clusters of little figures that would occasionally be obscured from view by drifting clouds of smoke. Some of them would fall down and not get up. Others would fall, get up again, run a little, crouch down, run again. Sometimes a man would throw out an arm before he fell, or fall backward and roll down the slope. I could usually tell when some of them got up near an enemy bunker. Then you'd see them moving sideways, looking for cover, kind of circling around as they tried to get close, and there would be these little puffs of black smoke from the grenades the North Koreans would toss out at them.

U.S. soldiers are positioned in a tunnel during combat at Heartbreak Ridge.

North Korea. These troops had been equipped by Stalin with tanks, artillery, and fighter jets. Now the United Nations Command forces were in retreat, eventually falling back across the 38th parallel. General MacArthur wanted to bring the war to China, including a massive invasion of Manchuria and the use of atomic bombs. Not wanting to extend the war beyond Korea's borders, Truman denied MacArthur's requests. The two men remained at odds until MacArthur's increasingly public criticism of Truman resulted in the president relieving the general of all his commands in April 1951. By then, the Korean War had ground to a halt, settling into a series of hill-by-hill battles that gained little ground but resulted in many casualties.

The American public had grown tired of hearing about American boys dying fighting Communists in a strange and faraway land. But overt protest was virtually nonexistent, and as the war continued, Americans were also occupied with reports of a new Communist threat much closer to home—inside their own government.

The Red Scare

Although membership in the Communist Party was not illegal in the United States, advocating the overthrow of the U.S. government was. By the late 1940s Communists in America had already been the subject of congressional hearings, media attacks, and criminal prosecution for their revolutionary views. A committee of the House of Representatives, the House Un-American Activities Committee (HUAC), had been formed in 1938 to investigate all types of subversive organizations. Gradually, the committee's focus had narrowed to investigating Communists. HUAC's probe of motion picture industry unions in 1947 led to the imprisonment of the "Hollywood Ten," a group of writers and directors, for their Communist leanings and refusal to reveal names for further investigations. Soon, the question "Are you now or have you ever been a member of the Communist Party?" echoed through the House chamber as hundreds of suspects were interrogated. Many people suspected of

being Communists were later "blacklisted" by radio and television networks and sponsors, and were unable to find work in an industry that shut them out in fear of being censured for hiring Communists.

Government, too, had its share of Communist witch-hunts. In 1948 Richard M. Nixon, then a congressman and later president of the United States, investigated an accusation that Alger Hiss, a former State Department official, had been a Communist spy in the 1930s. Hiss, a Democrat who had been an adviser to Franklin D. Roosevelt and was with the president at Yalta, protested that the charges were untrue and politically motivated. Nixon, a Republican, relentlessly pressed the investigation. He obtained damaging testimony from Whittaker Chambers, one of Hiss's former associates. Although Hiss could not be found guilty of espionage (the statute of limitations, or time limit, on the charge had run out), he was ultimately convicted of perjury, or lying under oath. In January 1950, Hiss was sentenced to five years in prison.

Throughout his trial, and in the years after his release from prison, Hiss maintained his innocence. And he had supporters in the government, including his friend Secretary of State Dean Acheson. When asked by reporters to comment on Hiss's conviction, Acheson said, "I should like to make it clear to you that whatever the outcome of any appeal

A Blacklisted Teacher

During the Communist witch-hunts of the late 1940s and early 1950s, many high-profile people in government and the entertainment industry were accused of being Communists. The loyalty of many other ordinary Americans was also being questioned by various anti-Communist groups. Frances Eisenberg, a California schoolteacher, was accused by the California State Committee on Un-American Activities of being a "skilled propagandist for Communist totalitarianism." In 1954 she was blacklisted, ending her nearly twenty-year teaching career. In *Red Scare: Memories of the American Inquisition* by Griffin Fariello, Eisenberg tells how her employer was pressured into firing her.

> The school administration knuckled under to the investigating committees and the board of education. They knew in advance that I was going to be fired. But I never was called in and asked "What are you teaching?" by anybody.

I was dismissed at a public meeting that the board held, crowded by my supporters. Police and plainclothesmen by the dozens in the hallway. When I exited from that room, a plainclothesman grabbed me by the shoulder and a policeman in uniform threw him aside and stood there beside me.

There were some loud voices of opposition there. As I sat there, I couldn't believe that after all those years of such devotion to my students and to my profession, I was being fired. I could no longer teach in the Los Angeles Unified School District. It was a shock.

(In 1986 a judge ruled the Los Angeles board of education's actions unconstitutional; Frances Eisenberg and four others received a total award of $250,000.)

which Mr. Hiss or his lawyers may take in this case, I do not intend to turn my back on Alger Hiss."[32] It was an extraordinary statement, a high government official voicing his support for a man convicted for lying about Communist activities. One man who took particular notice of it was a U.S. senator named Joseph R. McCarthy.

McCarthy's List

Joseph McCarthy was a little-known politician from Wisconsin. He had been a lawyer and a judge and had served with the U.S. Marines in the Pacific during World War II. He was elected to the U.S. Senate in 1947. But McCarthy will be remembered most for his claims that Communists had infiltrated the U.S. government. McCarthy's brazen accusations ruined lives and destroyed reputations and ultimately turned out to be totally unfounded.

By 1950 McCarthy's political career had been undistinguished, his tenure as a senator unremarkable. As reelection approached, he looked for an issue to spark his campaign, and he soon latched onto the question of communism in government. On February 9, 1950, McCarthy gave a speech in which he made the startling claim that he had proof of the Communist infiltration of Washington. As he spoke, the senator waved a piece of paper as his evidence. "I have here in my hand," McCarthy said, "a list of 205—a list of names that were made known to the Secretary of State as being members of the Communist Party and who nevertheless are still working and shaping policy in the State Department."[33] McCarthy repeated the charge to the press and in Congress, but when pressed to produce the list, he would not.

For the next several years, McCarthy searched for Communists in the U.S. government, using the malicious tactics of unsubstantiated charges, false information, and outright lies. The McCarthy witch-hunt ruined numerous careers by bestowing the label of "Communist" on innocent people. He even attacked George Marshall, the author of the Marshall Plan, as a traitor and Communist conspirator. But Senator Joseph McCarthy's reign of terror ended when he took on the U.S. Army.

"Point of Order"

In 1954, McCarthy accused the U.S. Army of security lapses and subversion involving alleged espionage at Fort Monmouth, New Jersey. The army, in turn, charged that the senator had sought preferential treatment for a young soldier formerly on his staff. The televised army-McCarthy Senate hearings began addressing the charges and counter-

charges in April 1954. During the nearly three-month-long hearings, McCarthy belligerently testified, belittling witnesses, introducing misleading evidence, and constantly interrupting the proceedings with cries of "Point of order!" But gradually the true nature of Joseph McCarthy was revealed to the Senate and to the American audience at home watching on television. Finally, Joseph Welch, the army's counsel, could stand McCarthy's bullying and smear tactics no longer. "You have done enough," Welch said to the senator. "Have you no sense of decency, sir, at long last? Have you left no sense of decency?"[34]

Senator McCarthy's long pursuit of Communists was over. Not one person he accused was ever proved to be a Communist threat to the government. McCarthy, censured by the Senate in 1954, never again wielded the unbridled influence he had during his Red-hunting days. He died three years later at the age of forty-eight. But his name lives on in the term given to the practice of false accusation and character assassination: McCarthyism.

Senator McCarthy saw Communist spies where there were none. But real spies did exist, and they operated secretly but effectively for both sides during the Cold War.

The Spy Game

Wars are fought on many levels, and the Cold War was no exception. Throughout

With the aid of a large map, Senator Joseph McCarthy makes his case against the U.S. army.

history, an important area of warfare has been the one designed to remain hidden: espionage, the art and science of gathering information about the enemy. During the Cold War, both the United States and the Soviet Union had large espionage organizations and networks of spies trying to uncover the secrets of the other side.

American espionage activities in World War II were handled by the Office of Strategic Services (OSS). When the war ended in 1945, the OSS was disbanded and its duties assumed by other government agencies. But over the next few years, the growing tensions between the United States and the Soviet Union emphasized the need for a single entity devoted to collecting vital information on potential enemies. In February 1947 Truman proposed the creation of a centralized intelligence-gathering group, and later that year Congress responded by passing the National Security Act. The act created an organization called the Central Intelligence Agency (CIA),

The Berlin Tunnel

In 1952, the CIA came up with the idea of gathering intelligence on Communist activities by tapping into communication cables buried under East Berlin. The Soviet military used these cables for transmitting important information by telephone and teletype. To intercept this information, CIA officers decided to dig a tunnel running from West Berlin to the Soviet eastern sector of the city.

After two years of secret planning, construction of the Berlin Tunnel began in February 1954, using the building of an army warehouse as a cover story. A year later, the nearly fifteen-hundred-foot-long tunnel was completed and wiretap and recording equipment installed. Over the next year, the CIA intercepted forty thousand hours of telephone conversations and 6 million hours of teletype traffic. But in April 1956 Soviet soldiers discovered the tunnel and broke through on the East Berlin side. They found the wiretaps and recording equipment but no American personnel.

Despite the discovery, the United States still had hours of useful Soviet information. Or did it? It was soon discovered that Soviet authorities had known about the entire tunnel project from the very beginning and that its "discovery" was a staged event. Was it possible that the Soviets had been sending false information, knowing that the Americans were listening in? The debate over the value of the tunnel information went on for years, but it was finally determined that most of the intelli-

gence gathered was genuine. The Soviets had learned about the Berlin Tunnel from a man named George Blake. A member of the British Secret Intelligence Service, he had attended a meeting in which the CIA informed the British about the tunnel. But Blake was in fact a "mole"—a Soviet spy who had secretly infiltrated British intelligence.

Soviet soldiers "discover" U.S. wiretaps in the Berlin Tunnel.

the first time an espionage agency had been formed to operate during peacetime.

The CIA's job was to gather, correlate, evaluate, and distribute to the proper government authorities information that might have an impact on national security. Beginning with just a few hundred people (many of them former OSS agents), the CIA had thousands of employees worldwide by 1952. During the early years of the Cold War, one of the CIA's major goals was to roll back communism, and it had several successes with covert operations in Third-World countries. In Iran in 1953 and Guatemala in 1954, the CIA brought about the overthrow of regimes tagged as Communist or anti-Western and installed governments favorable to the United States. These operations signaled a new kind of warfare that Americans would have to get used to. "There are no rules in such a game," warned a report on clandestine operations. "If the United States is to survive, long standing American concepts of 'fair play' must be reconsidered. We . . . must learn to subvert, sabotage and destroy our enemies by more clever, more sophisticated and more effective methods than those used against us."[35]

The CIA's successes in Iran and Guatemala helped stem the tide of Communist influence in the oil-rich Middle East and in Latin America. But the United States was not the only nation to conduct clandestine activities. The Soviet Union had a counterpart to the CIA in its own spy organization, the KGB.

Soviet Espionage

Since the Russian Revolution of 1917, the Soviet Union continuously conducted spy operations through a series of extensive and often quite successful espionage organizations. One of the biggest victories of Soviet espionage was the stealing of U.S. atomic bomb secrets. During World War II, Soviet spies, including British physicist Klaus Fuchs, infiltrated the Manhattan Project, America's program to build an atomic bomb. The top-secret information they stole eventually found its way to the Soviet Union, allowing the Russians to develop an atomic bomb years before they could have done so on their own.

Formed in 1954, the KGB (the Russian acronym for Committee on State Security) was the last in a long line of Soviet spy agencies. Unlike the CIA, the KGB's powers included domestic as well as foreign spying. During the Cold War, KGB agents operated covertly in the United States and Canada. In Great Britain, Soviet "moles" such as George Blake eventually infiltrated the highest levels of British intelligence and government. Many of these men had become Communists in the 1930s, when communism and a disdain for capitalist democracy was popular among young intellectuals at Cambridge University. Donald Maclean became first secretary of the British embassy in Washington and eventually gained access to the Atomic Energy Commission building. Kim Philby, the most successful double agent of the Cold War, operated at the top levels of British intelligence for years until he defected to Moscow, where he became an adviser to the head of the KGB.

At the midpoint of the twentieth century, the world had gone from postwar demobilization to an era of Cold War. A new armed conflict in far-off Asia, a Communist witch-hunt at home, and spies plying their trade under cover of secrecy were the hallmarks of a new and unsettling time. But the world was about to shift once more as the two superpowers, the United States and the Soviet Union, underwent transitions at the highest level of their governments.

The Cold War Expands

By 1952, Americans were beginning to wonder if the policy of containment was really working. Despite ongoing peace talks, the Korean War was bogged down in a bloody stalemate. The United States maintained its superiority in nuclear weapons, but the Soviet Union was closing the gap. Berlin remained a divided city, and Europe itself was still split by Churchill's Iron Curtain, a barrier that showed no signs of being lifted. As the elections of 1952 approached, President Harry Truman's popularity was waning. Disillusioned with the Korean stalemate, Americans began to look for a new president to direct the fight against communism. The man they ultimately chose had a winning smile and years of valuable experience in the art of waging war.

America Likes Ike

For an America in search of a new leader, Dwight D. Eisenhower seemed tailor-made for the job. Born in Texas and reared in a small town in Kansas, Eisenhower was a professional soldier who had graduated from the U.S. Military Academy at West Point in 1915. In a military career that spanned more than thirty years, he advanced to supreme commander of the Allied forces in Europe during World War II. Eisenhower's leadership of the D-day invasion on June 6, 1944, paved the way for the Allied victory that ended Hitler's Nazi regime.

Accepting the Republican Party's nomination for president in 1952, Dwight "Ike" Eisenhower easily defeated the Democratic candidate, Adlai E. Stevenson of Illinois. Richard M. Nixon, who as a congressman had pursued Communists a few years before, became Eisenhower's vice president. In addition to inheriting a newly renovated White House, Eisenhower also became heir to the challenges of fighting the Cold War.

During his campaign, Eisenhower had declared that he would go to Korea in order to see the war firsthand and to prepare for the job of ending it. "That job," Eisenhower said, "requires a personal trip to Korea. I shall make that trip. Only in that way could I learn how to best serve the American people in the cause of peace. I shall go to Korea."[36] Eisenhower's pledge was one of the main reasons for his election, and in December 1952 he made good on his promise. For three days, the president-elect toured the front lines, conferring with field commanders and eating meals with the troops. Upon his return to

the United States, Eisenhower considered various ways in which the war could be ended, including the use of nuclear weapons. But he decided to first attempt to get the stalled peace talks going again.

Talks of Peace

Peace talks between North Korean and Chinese delegates and UN representatives had begun on July 10, 1951, first at a town called

President Dwight Eisenhower (far left) shares a meal with U.S. soldiers during a visit to Korea.

Kaesong and later in Panmunjom. The talks continued on and off as the two sides argued over various negotiating points, eventually coming to an impasse over the location of the cease-fire line. In the summer of 1952, negotiations resumed only to halt once more in November over the disposition of prisoners of war. But Eisenhower soon noticed that the Communist negotiators had softened their demands concerning the prisoners, and talks resumed on April 26, 1953. Finally, on July 27, the armistice was officially signed and the Korean War was over.

More than 33,600 American soldiers died in combat during the Korean War, along with some 21,000 nonbattle deaths. More than 100,000 were wounded, and 3,700 American soldiers were held as prisoners of war. Millions of Koreans perished. But in the end, Korea remained, as it was before the war, divided at the 38th parallel, the north still controlled by Communists and the south remaining democratic. The United States now had a new commitment: to contain communism not only in Europe but in Asia as well.

The change in the Communist attitude in the peace negotiations had come as no surprise to President Eisenhower. For in March 1953 an event had occurred that would have an impact on the end of the Korean War and on the Cold War as well.

The Death of Stalin

Joseph Stalin had been the absolute dictator of the Soviet Union since 1929. He had brought Russia into the twentieth century by increasing his nation's industrial production. As an ally of the United States, he had helped defeat Adolf Hitler's Nazi regime in World War II. But Stalin's political advances were accompanied by a ruthless reign of terror that cost millions of Soviet citizens their lives. He had forcibly spread communism throughout the nations of Eastern Europe. And it was with his support that North Korea had invaded South Korea.

On March 4, 1953, President Eisenhower received word that Stalin had suffered a stroke and was in critical condition. The next day, a solemn report from Radio Moscow informed the world that Joseph Stalin was dead. Eisenhower realized that the impending change in Soviet leadership could herald a new era of trust and cooperation in U.S.-Soviet relations. He later recalled his thoughts during this hopeful time:

The new leadership in Russia, no matter how strong its links with the Stalin era, was not completely bound to blind obedience to the ways of a dead man. The future was theirs to make. Consequently, a major preoccupation of my mind through most of 1953 was the development of approaches to the Soviet leaders that might be at least a start toward the birth of a mutual trust founded in cooperative effort—an essential relationship between the two great powers, if they and other nations

The body of Soviet dictator Joseph Stalin lies in state in Moscow.

were to find the way to universal peace.[37]

Georgi Malenkov, a high-ranking member of Stalin's inner circle, became the new first secretary of the Communist Party (that is, the head of the party) and the leader of the Soviet government as premier of the Soviet Union. But within two weeks Malenkov resigned his position as party secretary, relinquishing the post to another party official, Nikita Khrushchev. A rumpled, rotund man who came from humble peasant stock, Khrushchev used his new position to become popular among local Communist Party officials across the Soviet Union. His advocacy of heavy industry won him followers in the Soviet army, and his program of increased agricultural production added to his influence.

As Khrushchev's support throughout the Soviet Union and at the highest levels of Soviet government grew, Malenkov's influence steadily weakened. On February 8, 1955, Georgi Malenkov resigned. A new premier, hand-picked by Khrushchev, initially replaced Malenkov, but by 1956 Khrushchev emerged as the undisputed head of the Communist Party and the Soviet Union. Thus, Nikita Khrushchev, a man of humble origins who had little formal education, became one of the most powerful figures of the Cold War. In a secret speech (which did not, however, remain secret for long) made at the Twentieth Party Congress in February 1956, Khrushchev called for the "de-Stalinization" of Russia, renouncing the terrorism and excesses that had marked the Stalin years. Khrushchev also advocated peaceful coexistence, or perhaps more accurately peaceful competition, between communism and capitalism. But despite the optimistic rhetoric, the superpowers' deep-seated view of each other as dangerous enemies would make the next years of the Cold War anything but peaceful, especially in the nations of Eastern Europe.

Khrushchev: Black and White

When Nikita Khrushchev took the reins of power in the Soviet Union, he was something of a mystery to Western political observers. Even Russians knew that there were two sides to the chubby dictator. Vladislav Zubok and Constantine Pleshakov, authors of *Inside the Kremlin's Cold War,* reflect on the dichotomy of Nikita Khrushchev.

> Nikita Khrushchev inherited the Cold War from Stalin, but his impact on its course was as legendary as his legacy in every aspect of Soviet life. His flamboyant personality, style, and beliefs help explain the most serious crises in U.S.-Soviet relations that held the world in suspense and finally brought it to the brink of war.
>
> It has long been said that there were two Khrushchevs: the ignorant and crude accomplice of Stalin's criminal system and the man of surprisingly human reactions. The Russian sculptor Ernst Niezvestny, who carved Khrushchev's face in stone on his grave, had one half of the face in white and the other half in black marble, symbolizing Khrushchev's light and dark sides. Khrushchev's role in the Cold War reflected these two sides: in him the revolutionary promise and the imperial, murderous legacy of Stalin were in constant conflict.

Nikita Khrushchev's personality sometimes baffled Western political observers.

Revolt in Hungary

At the end of World War II, the Soviet Union had liberated Hungary from the Nazis and installed a provisional government under Communist influence. By 1948, Hungary was firmly entrenched in the Soviet sphere of influence, with Matyas Rakosi, a ruthless follower of Stalin, as its premier. When Khrushchev came to power in the Soviet Union and de-Stalinization began, the future of Rakosi's repressive government looked uncertain at best. In July 1956 Rakosi was forced out of office and replaced by Erno Gero, a more moderate Communist. Soon, the citizens of Hungary were demanding that Soviet troops be removed from their country and that other reforms be instituted. Encouraged by a similar revolt in Poland, Hungarians took to the streets of their capital city.

October 23, 1956, was a cold, overcast day in Budapest. In the streets, a group of students and workers began protesting against the scarcity of food in Hungary and low wages paid to workers. What began as a small demonstration against the Communist leadership soon grew to a crowd of more than 100,000 roaming the streets and clashing with state security police. "It was a peaceful demonstration when it started," recalls reporter Endre Marton. "In hours it became a revolution; and in two days, it became a war. It was not planned—it was not organized. . . . It spread like a forest fire."[38]

Two days after the protests began, a former premier, Imre Nagy, was returned to office. Nagy promised to improve conditions and create a more democratic government. For a while, it seemed that the revolution would hold. But when the United Nations refused to support the revolutionaries and the United States offered no help other than some encouraging words, the Hungarian Revolution was doomed to failure. On November 4, Soviet tanks rolled into Budapest to put down the revolt. Citizens fought back with small arms and "Molotov cocktails," bombs made by pouring gasoline into a bottle and stuffing a cloth into the bottle's mouth for a fuse. But these meager weapons were no match for the Russian tanks. Within a week, the Hungarian Revolution had been crushed. Some 20,000 to 30,000 Hungarians lost their lives, and 200,000 more fled the country.

If the Hungarians thought the United States would come to their aid (as broadcasts from Radio Free Europe, an American radio service that transmitted pro-Western programs to Communist countries, seemed to imply), they were deeply disappointed. An opportunity to free an Eastern European nation seemed to slip by the Eisenhower administration, with disastrous results. "It was a tragedy," Richard Nixon later commented, "and a tragedy to which we contributed."[39] But another Cold War crisis was brewing, this time a technological one.

Angry Hungarians revolt against Communist leadership and the presence of Soviet troops.

The Nuclear Arsenal

At the end of World War II, the United States had been the only nuclear power, and the only nation to use that power during war. That monopoly ended in 1949 when the Soviet Union exploded its first atomic bomb. As an unprecedented arms race began to escalate, both nations sought to build more, and more powerful, weapons. In November 1952 the United States detonated the first hydrogen, or thermonuclear, bomb, a weapon more than five hundred times more powerful than the atomic bomb dropped on Hiroshima. But once again the American monopoly was short-lived. Less than a year later, in August 1953, the Soviet Union exploded its own hydrogen bomb.

The availability of such powerful weapons affected the way U.S. military leaders thought about future wars and how they would fight them. Maintaining a huge army and the tanks, artillery, and other necessary weapons to support it took a large portion of the federal budget. Fighting the Korean War, for example, had increased military spending more than 500 percent. To hold down expenses, Eisenhower, now in his second term as president, gave the military a "new look," reducing the number of conventional troops and placing an increased emphasis on nuclear weapons to defend the United States. The new look was both "a reallocation of resources," Eisenhower explained, and "the placing of greater emphasis than formerly on the deterrent and destructive power of improved nuclear weapons, better means of delivery, and ef-

President Eisenhower's military policy emphasized the deterrent use of weapons.

fective air-defense units."[40] Eisenhower's emphasis on the deterrent use of weapons was a major rationale for the Cold War arms race that followed. Successful nuclear deterrence meant that neither superpower would attack the other for fear of nuclear retaliation. As nuclear arsenals grew and became more deadly, deterrence would supposedly prevent any attack that could lead to all-out nuclear war.

In 1956 the U.S. supply of nuclear weapons, and the airplanes to deliver them, far outnumbered those in the Soviet Union. While the Soviet Union was frantically building more bombers, it was also trying to develop better methods of delivering nuclear payloads. The most promising of these new delivery technologies was the ballistic missile. Launched against an enemy in a high, arcing trajectory, a ballistic missile could deliver a nuclear bomb faster and more cheaply than a bomber could. Perhaps because of America's vast superiority in nuclear bombers, however, the U.S. military felt a false sense of security, and development of ballistic missiles for military use proceeded slowly and with little funding. But that security was shattered in October 1957 by tiny radio beeps from space.

Sputnik

Scientists in the Soviet Union had been hard at work since 1955 developing an intercontinental ballistic missile (ICBM), a rocket that could hurl their massive nuclear warheads a distance of five thousand miles. When they learned that the United

The launching of Sputnik (pictured), the first Russian space satellite, was a frightening milestone for Americans.

States was preparing a rocket to launch an artificial satellite into orbit around the earth, the scientists proposed that the Soviet Union use one of its missiles to launch its own satellite first. Premier Khrushchev appreciated the enormous propaganda value of beating America into space, so he approved a Soviet satellite project. After two test firings that summer, the Soviet Union launched the world's first artificial satellite into orbit on October 4, 1957. Named *Sputnik* ("fellow traveler" in Russian), the basketball-sized silver orb radioed a continuous "beep . . . beep . . . beep" back to earth. It was a sound that sent chills of dread into the American psyche.

Americans were astounded—and frightened—when they learned of the Soviet satellite. If the Russians had missiles powerful enough to put a satellite into orbit, could those same missiles be used to send a nuclear warhead to the United States? How could America, the world's technological leader, have been beaten by the Soviets? Journalists had similar questions for Eisenhower. When asked at a press conference if *Sputnik* represented a threat to national security, Eisenhower calmly expressed his confidence that the United States was safe. "As far as the satellite is concerned," the president told reporters, "that does not raise my apprehensions, not one iota. I can see nothing at this moment . . . that is significant in that development as far as security is concerned."[41]

But Khrushchev knew that the Soviet Union's ability to launch *Sputnik* tipped the Cold War balance of power. As he later wrote in his memoirs, "No longer was the industrial heartland of the United States invulnerable to our counterattack."[42] And in the United States itself, many people—government officials and citizens alike—did not share Eisenhower's confidence.

To many Americans, the underlying question posed by *Sputnik* was clear: Why was the United States falling behind the Soviet Union in science and technology? There was a scramble to place blame. One culprit, as proclaimed in numerous books, magazine articles, and television programs, was the American educational system, which was accused of failing its children and the country itself. Congress responded by passing the National Defense Education Act, a four-year, billion-dollar program to advance education, not only in science but in foreign languages, geography, and English as well. Funding for America's own satellite program was also increased.

On January 31, 1958, the United States launched its first satellite, named *Explorer,* from Cape Canaveral, Florida. Coming after the Soviet Union orbited a second *Sputnik* and a disastrous first attempt that ended in failure, the *Explorer* was a sign that the United States had finally entered the space race.

A Warning in Space

When the Soviet satellite *Sputnik* beeped its way into history, it had implications for the Cold War far greater than the basketball-sized orb that went into space: The same type of rocket that put *Sputnik* into orbit could also be used to launch nuclear missiles. Renowned British astronomer Sir Bernard Lovell used the sophisticated equipment at the Jodrell Bank observatory in England to observe radar images of *Sputnik*'s launch vehicle. The following recollection by Lovell is taken from *Inside the Cold War: An Oral History* by John Sharnik.

You could pick up the bleep-bleep from the *Sputnik* by a simple receiver. But the strength of our position [at Jodrell Bank observatory] was that we could give information about this rocket, which was an intercontinental missile, hurtling around in space. . . . After a few nights . . . we succeeded in locating the carrier rocket. It was a tremendous sighting. Nobody—certainly *we* had never seen what an echo from a missile looked like. And I very much doubt if anybody in the world did know what a radar echo from an intercontinental missile in orbit would look like. And it was quite spectacular. The [radar display] tube was full of the transient-meteor echoes; and then, suddenly, on the cathode ray tube, the echo from the carrier rocket appeared, a massive echo traveling in range along the orbit—unmistakenly something that had never been seen before. It showed us the Soviets could use a missile to land a weapon on the United States from Soviet territory. Just that. And at that time, it would not have been possible for the United States to have replied.

When President Eisenhower talked to the press after the *Sputnik* launch, his confidence that the Soviet Union posed no impending military threat to the United States was based on facts. But he could not tell reporters how he got those facts, because the information had been gathered by a secret Cold War technology: the spy plane.

Eyes in the Sky

It was a sleek, low-slung black aircraft, and after just one look, pilots dreamed of one day flying it. But only an elite few men would get to pilot the U-2, America's Cold War spy plane. Designed by Lockheed Martin Aircraft in 1954, the plane was designated U-2, or "Utility Two," a rather mundane name for such a striking design. With an eighty-foot wingspan measuring almost twice the length of its fuselage, the U-2 looked like a streamlined glider. But this "glider" was propelled by a powerful jet engine that could take it to more than seventy thousand feet. At that altitude, the U-2 was thought to be unreachable by Soviet missiles and could safely conduct its mission: to take spy photographs of the Soviet Union for the Central Intelligence Agency.

Russians survey the wreckage of the American U-2 spy plane piloted by Gary Powers.

Shootdown!

Francis Gary Powers was the pilot of the U-2 spy plane that was shot down over the Soviet Union on May 1, 1960. He recounts the moment his plane was hit by a Soviet missile in his book *Operation Overflight: The U-2 Spy Pilot Tells His Story for the First Time*. He had just turned his U-2 to make a course adjustment when the unthinkable happened.

Following the turn, I had to record the time, altitude, speed, exhaust-gas temperature, and engine-instrument readings. I was marking these down when, suddenly, there was a dull "thump," the aircraft jerked forward, and a tremendous orange flash lit up the cockpit and sky. . . . The orange glow seemed to last for minutes, although it was probably gone in seconds. Yet I had time enough to think the explosion external to the aircraft and, from the push, probably somewhere behind it.

The U-2 went into a spin, and soon Powers knew that he would have to get out of the aircraft. Procedure required that destruct switches had to be activated to destroy the U-2 so that it would not fall into Soviet hands. But when Powers loosened his safety harness, he was immediately pulled halfway out of the cockpit.

The aircraft was still spinning. I tried to climb back in to actuate the destruct switches, but couldn't; the *g* forces were too great. Reaching down, I tried to feel my way to the switches. I knew they were close, six inches away from my left hand at most, but I couldn't slip my hand under the windscreen to get at them. Unable to see, I had no idea how fast I was falling, how close to the ground. . . .

And then I thought: I've just got to try to save myself now. Kicking and squirming, I must have broken the oxygen hoses, because suddenly I was free, my body just falling, floating perfectly free. It was a pleasant, exhilarating feeling. Even better than floating in a swimming pool, I remember thinking.

I must have been in shock.

Beginning in 1956, U-2s of the CIA's Project Aquatone flew long-range, high-altitude reconnaissance missions over Eastern Europe, China, and the Soviet Union. The planes' high-resolution cameras snapped pictures of Soviet air bases, missile facilities, and industrial areas. Some twenty U-2s gathered valuable information about America's Cold War rival, including the fact that Russia's missiles were not yet advanced enough to pose a threat to the United States. Although most missions were successful, Eisenhower knew there was a possibility of a U-2 crashing in the Soviet Union. If that should happen, Eisenhower said, "the world would be in a terrible mess."[43] That possibility became a reality on May 1, 1960.

U-2 Down!

While preparing for a summit conference with the Soviet Union scheduled for May 16, 1960, Eisenhower was informed that a U-2 flown by CIA pilot Francis Gary Powers was overdue and presumed down. A cover story about a missing "weather reconnaissance" plane that had strayed off course was issued. But a few days later that cover story was blown when Premier Khrushchev announced that a U.S. spy plane had been shot down and that the pilot had been taken prisoner. Soon, photographs of Powers and pieces of the U-2 wreckage were put on display in the Soviet Union. Confronted with such indisputable and embarrassing evidence, Eisenhower had no choice but to take responsibility for the spy flights. "In the diplomatic field," Eisenhower later wrote, "it was routine practice to deny responsibility for an embarrassing occurrence . . . but when the world can entertain not the slightest doubt of the facts there is no point in trying to evade the issue."[44]

The CIA ended reconnaissance flights over the Soviet Union after the U-2 incident. Khrushchev canceled the scheduled summit meeting and re-scinded an invitation for Eisenhower to visit the Soviet Union. CIA pilot Powers was put on trial and convicted of espionage. He remained in a Soviet prison until February 1962, when he was traded for Colonel Rudolf Abel, a Soviet spy then in U.S. custody.

The U-2 incident was the last Cold War crisis that Dwight D. Eisenhower would face. As president for most of the 1950s, Eisenhower led the nation through an era of unprecedented prosperity and industrial growth. He confronted the Cold War head-on as it spread to new areas of international concern, from Asia to the Middle East, and played a role in the staggering increase in weapons of mass destruction. As the 1960s began, a charismatic young president would take the reins from the World War II generation and guide the nation toward a "New Frontier." No one could have predicted the uncertainty, turmoil, and fear that the next decade would bring.

Chapter 5

To the Brink of War

ohn F. Kennedy became the thirty-fifth president of the United States on January 20, 1961. On that cold, clear morning on the Capitol Plaza, the forty-three-year-old senator from Massachusetts stood bareheaded in the bright sunshine as he solemnly took the oath of office. Dwight D. Eisenhower stood nearby, the old soldier making way for the new president, the youngest man ever elected to the office. Kennedy, one of nine children from an influential Boston family, had served in the navy during World War II and was decorated for his heroic efforts to save his men when their PT boat was sunk.

In his inaugural address, Kennedy pledged that he was bringing to America not merely a new administration but a change of spirit and the enthusiasm of youth. "Let the word go forth," Kennedy declared, "from this time and place, to friend and foe alike, that the torch has been passed to a new generation of Amer-

John F. Kennedy's inauguration signaled a new generation of world leaders coming into prominence.

icans."[45] The new president also proclaimed to the world that the United States was ready to meet the challenges of the Cold War: "Let every nation know, whether it wishes us well or ill, that we shall pay any price, bear any burden, meet any hardship, support any friend, oppose any foe to assure the survival and the success of liberty. This much we pledge—and more."[46]

Just how much more would soon become clear.

Troubles with Cuba

On January 1, 1959, a little more than two years before John F. Kennedy's inauguration, a lean, bearded revolutionary named Fidel Castro seized power in Cuba, ousting the Caribbean island nation's corrupt dictator, Fulgencio Batista. Although he had promised to establish a democratic government in Cuba, Castro soon revealed his true political agenda: to create the first Communist nation in the Western Hemisphere. He denounced "Yankee imperialism," confiscated millions of dollars of American assets in Cuba, and forced Americans to flee the island. After imprisoning or executing his political opponents, Castro declared that he would turn to the Soviet Union for military assistance. On January 3, 1961, the United States broke off diplomatic relations with Cuba.

Alarmed by the idea of a Communist nation just ninety miles off the southern tip of Florida, President Eisenhower had devised a plan for CIA-trained Cuban exiles to invade Cuba and overthrow Castro. When Kennedy became president, he inherited Eisenhower's plans and ultimately decided to approve the invasion. The covert operation was scheduled for April 1961 at a point of entry called the Bay of Pigs. From the beginning the invasion was a fiasco; most of the exile force was captured or killed. The failed operation was an embarrassment for the new Kennedy administration and drove Castro further toward the Soviet Union.

A few months later, Cold War tensions would increase once more, this time in Europe, where a new obstacle would arise, literally, out of concrete and mortar.

Two Berlins

Berlin, a city that in the 1960s remained divided into Communist East and democratic West sectors, had become a symbol of the ideological split that defined the Cold War. To the people who lived in East Berlin, the division was more than just an abstract political idea, however, for life was very different on opposite sides of the city.

Conditions in the German Democratic Republic (GDR), or Communist East Germany, were typical of a Soviet-dominated society. Under the Communist system, wages were low, living conditions were poor, and food was expensive. Newspapers and radio broadcasts were heavily censored, and political dissent was harshly repressed.

Disaster at the Bay of Pigs

Situated on the southern coast of Cuba, the Bahía de Cochinos, or Bay of Pigs, was the location selected for an invasion designed to wrest control of Cuba from dictator Fidel Castro. The mission called for Cuban exiles trained by the CIA to land at the bay under cover of darkness and move swiftly through the countryside. Gaining recruits from local villages as they advanced, the rebel force, called Brigade 2506, would eventually topple Castro's regime. At least, that was the plan.

Two days before the attack, eight World War II vintage bombers lumbered through the skies over Cuban airfields. Flown by CIA-trained exile pilots, the bombers were to wipe out Castro's small air force in preparation for the invasion. Despite optimistic claims of planes destroyed, however, about half of Castro's air force remained untouched.

The actual invasion began on April 17, 1961, and from the beginning it was an utter disaster. Cuban patrols discovered the first wave of attackers as they hit the beach, thus eliminating the advantage of surprise. The exile troops soon found themselves pinned down on the beach by local militia units and soldiers of Castro's army. The remaining planes of Castro's air force attacked the troops on the beach and disabled their supply ship, depriving the landing forces of much-needed equipment and ammunition.

Despite the disasters that befell the rebel brigade, they still held out hope that the Americans would help. "I never saw the U.S. lose a war," brigade commander José Pérez San Román comments in *Inside the Cold War: An Oral History* by John Sharnik, "so I thought some mistake had happened and they were going to land later on. I thought they were going to come in and give us a hand until we were strong enough to continue by ourselves." But no U.S. aid was forthcoming, and by the third day the rebels realized that their assault had failed. More than one hundred Cuban exiles had been killed, and although some escaped into the Cuban hillside, most of those who survived were taken prisoner.

Unable to deny the obvious U.S. role in the Bay of Pigs fiasco, Kennedy took public responsibility for the botched operation and then promptly fired several top advisers. The new president's international reputation, as well as his self-confidence, was shaken, and the crisis remained a blot on the foreign relations record of his administration.

Comrades view the bodies of Cuban exiles slain in the disastrous Bay of Pigs invasion.

In contrast, democratic West Germany (the Federal Republic of Germany, or FRG) was on an economic upswing, aided by U.S. funding since the end of World War II. Intellectual freedom was allowed to blossom, cultural opportunities abounded, wages were high, and consumer goods were plentiful. Berlin, situated as it was deep inside Soviet-dominated East Germany, served as a microcosm of the struggle between freedom and subjugation and a showcase for capitalism. It is not surprising that many East Berliners, especially the young, crossed into West Berlin to escape the repression of the East for the freedom of the West. In the first half of 1961 alone, more than 150,000 people left East Berlin to start a new life in the West.

For Soviet premier Nikita Khrushchev, Berlin was a "bone in the throat"[47] of his empire. At a summit conference with President Kennedy in Vienna, Austria, June 1961, Khrushchev vowed to conclude a treaty that would end Western influence in East Germany. But first he had to prevent the further exodus of East Berliners. He did so by the most blunt means. One

Friends and families wave to each other over the Berlin Wall, which was erected in August, 1961.

morning in August 1961, Berliners awoke to the jarring sounds of bulldozers and jackhammers. Khrushchev had ordered the construction of a wall separating East and West Berlin. Once completed, the Berlin Wall, topped with barbed wire and guarded by armed Soviet troops, prevented East Berliners from escaping to the West and effectively isolated West Berliners from their friends and relatives in the East. More than ever, Berlin was held up as a symbol of Cold War divisions.

In 1961 President Kennedy, still haunted by the Bay of Pigs fiasco, decided that the building of the Berlin Wall was not a sufficient provocation by the Communists to risk a war. But in October 1962 the Soviet Union made a move that brought the world to the brink of nuclear holocaust. And it centered once again on the island nation of Cuba.

Early Warning

In the late summer of 1962, some disturbing information began to reach the United States from intelligence sources inside Cuba. During the past several months, an increasing number of cargo

The Wall

Shortly after midnight on August 13, 1961, soldiers took up positions as bulldozers and Soviet-made tanks lumbered through the streets of Berlin. Under the glare of powerful floodlights, workmen erected concrete posts and began stringing rolls of barbed wire along the East Berlin–West Berlin border. Rail traffic was halted and streets between the sectors were blocked. The Brandenburg Gate—the main access point between East and West Berlin—was heavily guarded by tanks, troops, and machine guns. On orders from Soviet premier Khrushchev, Berlin was being sealed off from the Western world.

By the end of the day, the crude barbed wire barrier separating East and West Berlin was complete. This initial barricade was only temporary; but construction of a permanent concrete wall would begin four days later. Temporary or not, the barrier produced the desired effect for Khrushchev: Access to the West, to its theaters, shops, and jobs, was denied to the citizens of East Berlin.

Over the next several months, a more permanent Berlin Wall was constructed by East German workers under the watchful eyes of armed guards. Eventually more than ninety miles long, it was an ugly barrier of concrete, barbed wire, and guard towers that completely isolated West Berlin. Arthur M. Schlesinger Jr., a special assistant to President Kennedy, describes a 1962 visit to the Berlin Wall in *A Thousand Days: John F. Kennedy in the White House:*

> After breakfast we made a tour of the Wall. It was more barbaric and sinister than one could have imagined—the crude, gray concrete blocks, the bricked-in windows of apartment houses along the sector line, the vicious tank traps, the tall picket fences erected to prevent East Berliners from even waving to relatives or friends in West Berlin, the plain white crosses marking places where people had jumped to their death.

LAUNCH POSITION

MISSILE-READY TENTS

MISSILE ERECTORS

A photograph taken from a U-2 spy plane shows intricate details of a Cuban missile base.

shipments from Russia to Cuba had been observed by U.S. reconnaissance aircraft. Now, reports were beginning to circulate of military construction being undertaken on the island. In addition, thousands of Russian technicians and dozens of Soviet missiles had been discovered inside Cuba. These missiles were defensive weapons designed to shoot down enemy aircraft, and their installation in Cuba worried the Kennedy administration. What other, potentially more dangerous, weapons might the Soviets be planning to deploy? The United States had to find out.

Big Missiles in Cuba

On October 14, 1962, a lone U-2, its secret mission code-named Victor, streaked across the clear skies over western Cuba. From an altitude of seventy thousand feet, the aircraft snapped hundreds of photographs of the Cuban countryside far below with its high-resolution camera, then sped to McCoy Air Force Base in Orlando, Florida. The mission was, in the pilot's own words, "a piece of cake—a milk run,"[48] and there had been no challenges from Soviet missiles.

The next day, October 15, expert photo interpreters at the National Photographic Interpretation Center in Washington, D.C., were busy analyzing the U-2's film with high-power magnifiers. The interpreters soon discovered several long canvas-covered objects on the ground near the town of San Cristóbal. These were identified as offensive missiles with a range of about twelve hundred miles, well within the targeting distance of Atlanta, Houston, and Washington, D.C. One of the photo interpreters announced the alarming news to his supervisor with one terse sentence: "We've got big missiles in Cuba."[49]

ExComm

McGeorge Bundy, assistant to the president for national security, told Kennedy about the missiles in Cuba on the morning of October 16. The president remained calm as Bundy recounted the photographic evidence obtained by the U-2, but he was angry that Khrushchev would install offensive weapons while assuring the United States that any military buildup in Cuba would be only defensive in nature. At a news conference just a month before, Kennedy had stated, "If at any time the Communist build-up in Cuba were to endanger or interfere with our security in any way . . . or if Cuba should ever . . . become an offensive military base of significant capacity for the Soviet Union, then this country will do whatever must be done to protect its own security and that of its allies."[50] To decide what it was that "must be done," Kennedy called for the formation of a committee to meet later that morning.

The Executive Committee (ExComm), made up of the president and top military and government officials, convened in the Cabinet Room of the White House for the first of what would be many meetings. Blowups of the U-2 photographs were displayed; after examining them, Kennedy asked the crucial question: "How long will it be before they can fire those missiles?"[51] Experts estimated that the missiles could be operational within a few weeks. There was no time to waste. Kennedy ordered more reconnaissance overflights of Cuba, including low-altitude flights that could take more detailed photographs than the high-altitude U-2s.

Over the next several days, ExComm met to examine new photographic evidence and discuss the U.S. response to the missiles in Cuba. Several options were considered, including launching air strikes targeted at the missile sites, a full-scale invasion of Cuba to destroy the missiles and topple the Castro government, and a naval blockade to stop any further missiles from reaching Cuba. Or the United States could simply do nothing and see what developed. Each plan had its dangers. A military attack on Cuba would provoke a response from the Soviet Union, most likely in Berlin, which could trigger World War III. On the other hand, doing nothing would make the United States appear weak willed and allow the military buildup in Cuba to proceed unhindered. Finally, after exhaustive deliberations, late on Thursday, October 18, a tentative decision was made. Whether it would end the crisis or lead to war, no one on the committee knew.

Quarantine

Although some members of ExComm still favored an air strike, the final decision was officially made by President Kennedy on Saturday, October 20: The United States would establish a naval blockade in which all ships bound for Cuba would be stopped and searched. If weapons or other military equipment were found, the ships would be turned back. Although less drastic than an air strike or invasion, a naval blockade was nonetheless fraught with danger. What would happen if a ship refused to stop?

What about the possibility of an accidental collision? Any incident between U.S. and Soviet ships might touch off an armed exchange that could lead to all-out war. In one small effort to keep the plan peaceful, the word *quarantine* was used instead of *blockade,* a term that denotes an act of war.

On Monday night, October 22, 1962, President John F. Kennedy went on television and radio to explain the crisis to the public. Until then, the Soviet missiles in Cuba and U.S. plans for dealing with them had been kept under strictest secrecy to avoid possible panic. But now the American people—and the world—had to know. At 7:00 P.M. Kennedy faced three television cameras in the Oval Office and began the most important speech of his presidency: "Good evening, my fellow citizens."[52] For the next seventeen minutes, Kennedy described the discovery of the missiles in Cuba and the quarantine that would be the U.S. response. In a calm voice, he explained that he was placing U.S. troops on alert, and warned that any missile launched from Cuba against any nation in the Western Hemisphere would be considered an attack on the United States by the Soviet Union itself.

Military preparations for the quarantine and possible armed conflict had already been set in motion. Around the world, U.S. forces were at Defense Condition 3 (DEFCON 3), a heightened state of military readiness. U.S. missile silos and nuclear bombers were on alert, and submarines carrying nuclear missiles prepared their deadly payloads for action. U.S. Navy ships had left their berths and were headed out into the Atlantic Ocean with Russian-speaking interpreters on board. The world inched closer to a superpower confrontation.

And while President Kennedy was still delivering his speech under the hot television lights in the Oval Office, nineteen Soviet cargo ships were steaming across the Atlantic, bound for Cuba.

"Eyeball to Eyeball"

The quarantine officially went into effect at 10:00 A.M. on Wednesday, October 24, 1962. The quarantine line was established in an arc five hundred miles from Cuba, and U.S. warships were ready to intercept any Soviet vessels that tried to cross it. In Washington, Ex-Comm met to discuss the latest intelligence reports. The news was not good.

A U.S. patrol plane flies threateningly low over a Soviet freighter off the coast of Cuba.

President Kennedy announces plans for a naval blockade to keep additional missiles from reaching Cuba.

Further aerial reconnaissance flights over Cuba had confirmed that the work on the Soviet missile sites was proceeding without interruption. In the CIA's opinion, some of the missiles were now operational, although it was not known if they carried nuclear warheads.

The one piece of good news to reach ExComm was that the Soviet ships heading for the quarantine line were slowing down, and some had even turned back toward the Soviet Union. Taking this as a sign that the crisis might be easing, Secretary of State

Dean Rusk commented, "We're eyeball to eyeball and I think the other fellow just blinked."[53] Yet even this good news was tempered by uncertainty. Were the Soviet ships really going home? Or were they possibly regrouping to prepare for a run at the quarantine line? Kennedy desperately wanted to avoid a showdown with the Soviet military, but such a conflict was a distinct possibility. Rusk told the president, "Our commanders have been instructed to avoid hostilities if at all possible, but this is what we must be prepared for, and this is what we must expect."[54] As if to reinforce Rusk's comments, for the first time in history the U.S. military went to DEF-CON 2. It was the alert status just short of all-out war.

While the military was preparing for war, the Kennedy administration was desperately trying to devise a diplomatic solution to the crisis.

Negotiating for Peace

In the 1960s instant satellite communications and the worldwide reach of the Internet were still years in the future. Diplomacy was handled, as it had been for hundreds of years, by letters, telegrams, and face-to-face meetings. On October 26, 1962, President Kennedy received a letter from Premier Khrushchev stating that if the United States promised never to invade Cuba, then the Soviet Union would remove its missiles from the island. To ExComm, it appeared that Khrushchev was looking for a way to end the missile crisis without risking military action.

The next day, October 27, another letter from Khrushchev arrived in Washington. Unlike Khrushchev's first letter, sent privately to President Kennedy, this one was also broadcast publicly from Radio Moscow. In it, Khrushchev's tone had become more hostile, and he had

changed his demands. Now, he said, in order to secure the dismantling of the missiles from Cuba, the United States must remove its missiles located in Turkey, on the Soviet Union's southwestern border. Turkey was a NATO nation, and U.S. missiles had been in place there for years as a protective measure for the nearby NATO nations of Europe. Removing them could give a signal that the United States was pulling back on its commitment to defend Europe. In fact, the missiles in Turkey were obsolete, and the United States was considering eliminating them anyway. But to do so now, at the height of the crisis, would make the United States look like it was bowing to Khrushchev's demands.

After long hours of sometimes heated discussion, the committee decided to reply to Khrushchev's offer stated in his *first* letter, instead of to the more belligerent second one. This would allow the United States to get the Soviet missiles out of Cuba by simply pledging not to invade. As for the U.S. missiles in Turkey, a secret deal was made by Robert Kennedy, the president's brother and U.S. attorney general. Meeting with Soviet ambassador Anatoly Dobrynin, "Bobby" Kennedy assured him that in a short time after the crisis was over, the missiles based in Turkey would be gone.

Once the president's response had been sent to Khrushchev, all that Ex-Comm, and the world, could do was wait.

"Ich bin ein Berliner"

In June 1963 President John F. Kennedy made a goodwill tour of Europe. His first stop on that journey was Germany, where, on June 26, he spoke to a huge crowd that thronged the Rudolf Wilde Platz. In the shadow of the Berlin Wall, Kennedy addressed the cheering, waving masses with a memorable speech, a portion of which appears here, taken from Arthur M. Schlesinger's book *A Thousand Days: John F. Kennedy in the White House.*

There are many people in the world who really don't understand, or say they don't, what is the great issue between the free world and the Communist world.

Let them come to Berlin!

There are some who say that communism is the wave of the future.

Let them come to Berlin!

And there are some who say in Europe and elsewhere we can work with the communists.

Let them come to Berlin!

And there are even a few who say that it is true that communism is an evil system, but it permits us to make economic progress.

Lass sie nach Berlin kommen! Let them come to Berlin!

A few moments later, Kennedy concluded his speech with a historic phrase:

All free men, wherever they may live, are citizens of Berlin, and, therefore, as a free man, I take pride in the words *"Ich bin ein Berliner."* ["I am a Berliner."]

Stepping Back from Danger

The next morning, October 28, 1962, Khrushchev's reply was ready. Considering the gravity of the situation and the time it would take to send a personal message to President Kennedy, the Soviets broadcast the response over Radio Moscow. The message proclaimed that the Soviets would begin dismantling their missiles in Cuba and transporting them back to the Soviet Union, under the supervision of the United Nations. At 11:00 A.M., ExComm met and drafted a reply from President Kennedy to Khrushchev. "I think that you and I," Kennedy wrote to the Soviet premier, "with our heavy responsibilities for the maintenance of peace, were aware that developments were approaching a point where events could have become unmanageable. So I welcome this message and consider it an important contribution to peace."[55] He concluded that there was still much progress to be made in the field of disarmament. "Perhaps now, as we step back from danger, we can together make real progress in this vital field."[56] It would take years and many false starts for that progress to be realized. But for now it was enough that a crisis had been ended, and a nuclear war averted.

Aftermath

Not everyone was pleased with the outcome of the Cuban Missile Crisis. In Cuba, Premier Fidel Castro felt that his country had been betrayed by the Soviets, who, upon pulling their missiles out, would leave Cuba open to invasion by the United States. And, indeed, many American military leaders felt that the United States ought to invade Cuba and overthrow Castro, despite the settlement of the crisis. But cooler heads in Washington prevailed, and the powerful United States never invaded the small island of Cuba.

Throughout the next several weeks, aerial reconnaissance photographs showed that the Cuban missile sites were being dismantled and the missiles loaded onto cargo ships for transport back to the Soviet Union. On November 20, President Kennedy directed that the naval quarantine be officially lifted. Although the crisis was over, Cuba, and its bellicose leader Castro, remained a thorn in America's side.

As a result of the nuclear "close call," relations between the United States and the Soviet Union warmed somewhat. Realizing that the old methods of communication were dangerously slow in a time of international crisis, a "hot line" was established between Washington and Moscow to speed important messages between the superpowers. In 1963 a limited nuclear test ban treaty was agreed upon by the United States, the Soviet Union, and Great Britain. All atmospheric, outer space, and underwater testing of nuclear weapons was banned. Also in 1963 the United States quietly removed its missiles from Turkey.

President Kennedy (right) talks with his brother, Attorney General Robert Kennedy, who represented America in talks with the Soviets.

President Kennedy had confronted the Soviets at the brink of nuclear war and had brought the world safely back from that brink. It was the finest hour in his tragically short presidency. On November 22, 1963, Kennedy was killed by an assassin while riding in a motorcade in Dallas, Texas. That same day, Lyndon B. Johnson, Kennedy's vice president, took the oath of office on the presidential airplane, Air Force One. For the new president, the nation was heading into a new phase of the Cold War. Whereas his predecessor had avoided a world war, Johnson would become embroiled in a different kind of war, one that would drag on longer than any other American conflict.

Chapter 6

The Vietnam Era

The destroyer USS *Maddox*, under the command of Captain John Herrick, sailed slowly through the calm waters of the Gulf of Tonkin, a few miles off the coast of the Southeast Asian nation of Vietnam. It was August 2, 1964, and the *Maddox* was on a secret intelligence-gathering mission. Soviet radar equipment and antiaircraft missiles were being positioned along the coast of North Vietnam, and the United States needed information on these new installations. At about 11:00 A.M., radar operators on the *Maddox* detected three small patrol boats heading at high speed toward the destroyer. Captain Herrick ordered his gunners to be ready to repel an imminent attack. As the small boats closed in, they launched torpedoes, which either missed the *Maddox* or were duds. Then the destroyer's guns opened fire, disabling two of the boats and sinking the third. The skirmish lasted only twenty minutes, but it had far-reaching consequences.

Three days later, President Lyndon Johnson sent the Gulf of Tonkin Resolution to Congress for approval. This resolution, which Congress passed by an overwhelming majority, empowered the president "to take all necessary measures to repel any armed attack against the forces of the United States and to prevent further aggression."[57] Although it was not a formal declaration of war, Johnson now had nearly unlimited authority to wage war in Vietnam. The Cold War was heating up again, and, as with Korea in the 1950s, young men were about to be sent into combat thousands of miles away. As Americans watched television news reports, they wondered why the United States was so interested in a far-off nation like Vietnam.

Vietnam's Strategic Importance

Vietnam lies along the eastern coast of the Indochinese Peninsula, which juts into the South China Sea between India and China. Since the arrival of French missionaries in Southeast Asia in the seventeenth century, France had exerted an influence on Vietnam. By the mid-1800s, French military forces were providing protection for the missionaries against local opposition. In 1887 Vietnam and its neighbors Cambodia and Laos became a French colony called French Indochina. After World War II, France struggled to maintain its hold on Vietnam against the Vietminh, a nationalist organization formed by Communist leader Ho Chi Minh dedicated to creating an independent Vietnam.

In 1950 the Soviet Union and China formally recognized the Communist government of Ho Chi Minh. That same year the United States began sending military aid to the French in Vietnam, hoping to prevent the country from falling to Ho Chi Minh's Communist forces. It was another step in America's policy to contain communism, and an acknowledgment of a new principle called the "domino theory." This theory stated that if Vietnam fell to the Communists, the rest of Southeast Asia would eventually follow one by one, like a row of dominoes being toppled. Although some dismissed this idea, the United States nevertheless increased its financial aid to the French in Vietnam. Still, France was having trouble defeating Ho Chi Minh, a tenacious enemy who years earlier had boasted, "You can kill ten of my men for every one I kill of yours. But even at those odds, you will lose and I will win."[58] Ho made good on his boast in May 1954 when the French were defeated in a fierce battle at the town of Dien Bien Phu. Subsequent negotiations divided Vietnam into two parts, Communist North Vietnam and an independent, non-Communist South Vietnam. Like Korea, Vietnam was now a divided nation. Although the split was meant to be temporary, to last only until elections could be held, Vietnam would remain divided for more than twenty years.

The United States Takes Over

After its defeat at Dien Bien Phu, France's influence in Vietnam declined,

The Vietnam War

North Vietnam
South Vietnam

Henry Kissinger: A Realistic Diplomat

In September 1973 President Richard Nixon selected the first man born in a foreign country to be a U.S. secretary of state. But by the time of his appointment, Henry Kissinger had already become a vital agent of American diplomacy.

Henry Kissinger was born in 1923 in Fürth, Germany, the first son of Jewish parents. He came to the United States in 1938 when his family left Germany to escape the Nazi persecution of Jews. The Kissingers settled in New York, where Henry attended City College. In 1943, nineteen-year-old Henry entered the U.S. Army, where he served in counterintelligence in Germany. After the war, Kissinger returned home to earn a doctorate at Harvard University.

Kissinger first gained fame as an expert on international relations with the publication of his best-selling book *Nuclear Weapons and Foreign Policy* in 1957. He was a part-time consultant on foreign policy for both the Kennedy and Johnson administrations, and in 1968 president-elect Nixon made Kissinger his assistant for national security affairs. Although earlier Kissinger had expressed doubts about Nixon's ability to handle the presidency, these two very different men found they were able to work together. The intellectual Kissinger forged a more realistic approach to foreign policy for the United States, stressing areas of cooperation with the Soviet Union rather than rabid anticommunism. Kissinger used secret back-channel negotiations to help establish the foundations of détente, to pave the way for Nixon's historic trip to China, and to bring about an end to the Vietnam War. He continued as secretary of state under Nixon's successor, Gerald R. Ford.

In September 1973, just a month after the U.S. Senate confirmed Kissinger as secretary of state, he was awarded the Nobel Peace Prize for negotiating the cease-fire in Vietnam. He shared the prize with Le Duc Tho, the chief North Vietnamese negotiator. But with fighting still going on in Vietnam, Le Duc Tho refused to accept the honor, and Kissinger made an excuse for not attending the ceremony in Norway. Two years later, when Saigon fell to the Communists, Kissinger offered to return the medal. The Nobel committee refused his offer.

and by 1956 all French troops had been pulled out. That left the South Vietnamese army (the Army of the Republic of Vietnam, or ARVN) to carry on the fight against communism. At that point, the United States already had several hundred military "advisers" in Vietnam, officially there to train the ARVN troops in how to use American-supplied weapons. That number steadily increased over the next several years; by the time Lyndon Johnson became president, more than sixteen thousand U.S. soldiers were stationed in South Vietnam. When Congress approved Johnson's Gulf of Tonkin Resolution in 1964, it was a signal that the war was about to escalate. But neither the president nor the American people knew what was in store both in Vietnam and at home.

Communist guerrillas known as Vietcong had spread throughout South Vietnam, raiding ARVN installations and attacking U.S. troops as well. These successes were made possible by the Soviet and Chinese backing the Vietcong received. As these incidents increased in frequency and severity (due to the Vietcong's Soviet-made weapons, delivered through China), more and more American casualties were reported. After two Vietcong attacks on U.S. military bases in South Vietnam, President Johnson initiated Operation Rolling Thunder in March 1965, a campaign of continuous bombing of North Vietnam by the air force and navy that would continue for three years. But it soon became clear to President Johnson and his military commander in Vietnam that an air war alone would not defeat the Communists. In a televised address broadcast on July 28, 1965, Johnson told the American people, "I have asked the commanding general, General [William] Westmoreland, what more he needs to meet this mounting aggression. He has told me. And we will meet his needs. We cannot be defeated by force of arms. We will stand in Vietnam."[59]

General William Westmoreland (seated) inspects a base camp in Vietnam.

Escalation

What General Westmoreland needed to prevent the collapse of South Vietnam was a U.S. combat force on the ground. Johnson agreed, and by the end of 1965 nearly 200,000 U.S. troops were stationed in Vietnam. While the bombing of North Vietnam continued over the next two years, U.S. troop strength in Vietnam would dramatically increase. By December 1967, U.S. forces in Vietnam numbered almost a half-million soldiers, both combat troops and logistical support personnel. A million tons of supplies were being delivered every month to support the growing number of soldiers. Aircraft of every description, from buzzing helicopters to thundering B-52 bombers, filled the skies over Vietnam. U.S. naval vessels navigated the South China Sea off Vietnam's coast and patrolled the muddy rivers inland. But as the number of U.S. troops in Vietnam increased, so did the number of U.S. casualties. By the end of 1967, more than 16,600 Americans had been killed in action in Vietnam. And the worst year was yet to come.

Faced with a war that had no front lines and an enemy that seemed to appear out of nowhere and disappear just as quickly, the United States soon found it-

Police arrest a protester in Chicago during a rally against the Vietnam War.

self mired in a conflict different from any other it had ever fought. And as U.S. casualties mounted, so did protests against the war back home.

The War at Home

During the 1950s, Americans had become somewhat used to, if not completely comfortable with, living in a world dominated by the Cold War. Although the thought of nuclear annihilation lingered in the back of most Americans' minds, the life and death struggles of the Cold War usually occurred thousands of miles away, in places like Berlin and Poland. But in the 1960s, thousands of young men began leaving the United States bound for Southeast Asia. And before long, many began returning home in flag-draped coffins. Vietnam changed forever Americans' views about war, the government, and the morality of fighting communism in a far-off land. This was due in no small part to the fact that, on any particular night, scenes of the Vietnam War were delivered into America's homes by television.

Unlike in previous wars, in which people got news of victories and defeats from newspapers or radio, television brought an unprecedented immediacy to the fighting in Vietnam. Night after night, Americans turned on their TV sets to watch graphic wartime images from halfway around the world. But television also showed scenes of unrest at home as demonstrators, mostly college students,

took to the streets to protest the war, not always peacefully. From antiwar "teach-ins" organized early in the war to draft-card-burning rallies and peace marches, many of America's youth registered their opposition to the Vietnam War and clashed with police charged with keeping order. In time, antiwar sentiment and disillusionment with American government would spread to academia, major media, and even mainstream America.

With so much attention focused on the war in Southeast Asia and protests at home, it seemed all too easy to forget about America's traditional Cold War adversary. But the Soviet Union, as the world's other superpower, was still a major factor in the Cold War.

U.S.-Soviet Relations in the 1960s

Glassboro is a small town in southern New Jersey, located about halfway between New York City and Washington, D.C. Renowned during the Revolutionary Era for its glassmaking industry (which gave the town its name), Glassboro became the site of a two-day summit meeting between the leaders of the Cold War superpowers, President Lyndon Johnson and Soviet premier Aleksei Kosygin, in June 1967. Kosygin was a member of the Soviet ruling troika, or three-man collective, which had come to power after Nikita Khrushchev was forced out of office in October 1964. Among the subjects the two heads of state discussed in the two meetings were the Vietnam War and U.S.

reaction to the recent armed clash be-tween Arab and Israeli forces known as the Six Day War. But the most important topic of discussion, and the one that posed the gravest global threat, was the proliferation of nuclear arms. Ever since the Soviet Union detonated its first atomic bomb in 1949, the arms race be-tween the United States and the Soviet Union had been steadily escalating in the numbers of bombs, missiles, and war-heads that each side possessed. The talks at Glassboro were important because U.S.-Soviet relations played a role in all of these issues.

The summit meeting between the two leaders was cordial. Johnson later characterized Kosygin as "an extremely intelligent and competent person with a personal capacity for humor and human feeling."[60] But the Soviet premier was tough when it came to the details of the meetings. Concerning Vietnam, Kosygin bluntly declared that the United States should stop the bombing of North Viet-nam and withdraw its combat troops. Johnson replied that it was the Soviet weapons used by the North Vietnamese army and the Vietcong that were pro-longing the war. Kosygin predicted re-newed conflicts in the Middle East as a result of the Six Day War, including the possibility of a U.S.-Soviet confrontation. When the discussion turned to the arms race, Kosygin said that as long as the Vietnam and Middle East conflicts con-tinued, disarmament would have to wait.

The Glassboro summit resulted in no new agreements between the United States and the Soviet Union. But at least a seed of cooperation in slowing the spread of nu-clear weapons was sown between the two leaders. According to an official report on the summit, "It is perfectly clear that they [the Soviets] want a non-proliferation treaty if they can get one."[61] Yet President Johnson knew that the road to mutual un-derstanding would be a long one, and the two meetings at Glassboro were just the be-ginning. "With Russians," he said, "it takes three meetings to make a deal: the first, courteous; the second, rough; the third, the deal is made. . . . The third session will not be a single session. It will consist in what unfolds in the weeks and months ahead on the specific issues and positions I took up with the Chairman."[62]

Regardless of the beginnings of a new understanding between the superpowers, the United States was still occupied by the war in Southeast Asia. The year 1968 would turn out to be the worst year in the seemingly endless quagmire of Vietnam. And it began with a deadly surprise of-fensive by the Vietcong.

The Tet Offensive

Tet is the traditional Vietnamese lunar New Year, which is celebrated over sev-eral days beginning on January 30. As 1968 began, the Vietcong, the United States, and the Army of the Republic of Vietnam negotiated a thirty-six-hour truce in honor of the new year. Thou-

U.S. soldiers in a beach assault during the Tet Offensive, a victorious but costly battle for the United States.

sands of Vietnamese soldiers went home to be with their families, to celebrate and exchange gifts for the holiday. It was intended to be a peaceful respite in the midst of the war.

Shortly after midnight on January 30, the peace was shattered by the sounds of mortars, rockets, and rifle fire. Some eighty thousand Vietcong had begun a massive and coordinated assault all across South Vietnam. Concentrating on urban areas, the Vietcong attacked over one hundred cities, towns, and villages, including the South Vietnamese capital of Saigon and the historic city of Hué. In Saigon, the U.S. embassy was attacked by a Vietcong

commando squad, which managed to kill several U.S. soldiers before being defeated. Caught off-guard by this brazen violation of the Tet truce, U.S. and ARVN forces nevertheless fought back and, after more than a month of fighting, repulsed the Vietcong invasion. The Communists had hoped that the invasion would spark a popular uprising among the South Vietnamese. What resulted instead was a failed invasion and more than thirty thousand Communist casualties.

Although it was a military victory for the United States, the Tet Offensive proved to be a public relations disaster for President Johnson.

The Credibility Gap

As Americans watched battles in Vietnam unfold on television, their opinions on the war and the government leaders who were running it began to change. Before the Tet Offensive, General William Westmoreland, at the urging of President Johnson, had proclaimed to the press that "we have reached an important point when the end begins to come into view."[63] But television showed a war that was anything but winding down. Such discrepancies between official statements and the reality of the war

A Protest in Washington

The Vietnam War was fought not only in the jungles of Southeast Asia but also on campuses and in the streets of America. The following account of a mass protest in Washington, D.C., that occurred in October 1967 is taken from the book *1968*, by Clark Dougan and Stephen Weiss.

As the last speeches came to an end at the Lincoln Memorial, 30,000 demonstrators linked arms, crossed the Arlington Memorial Bridge, and advanced toward the Pentagon. They came, said a spokesman for the Episcopal Peace Fellowship, "to disrupt the center of the American war machine." Suddenly, hundreds of young people broke through a line of MPs [military police] and raced up the Pentagon's main steps. As thousands more followed, troops fired tear gas and struck the demonstrators with truncheons. A second charge carried a few protesters into the building before a wave of soldiers hurled them out. For the rest of the afternoon the demonstrators alternately taunted the troops in front of them and cajoled the soldiers to "join us." In the early October twilight someone held aloft a burning draft card; soon hundreds of such tiny flames flickered in the darkness. At midnight, after reporters had left, soldiers and federal marshals began clubbing those protesters directly in front of the main entrance and hauling them away. By the time the demonstration came to an end twenty-four hours later, more than 700 people had been arrested and fully twice that number listed as casualties.

were known as the "credibility gap," and it caused further problems for Johnson. After Tet, the president's approval rating plummeted, and only about one in four Americans agreed with Johnson's handling of the war. Criticism of the president in the media also increased. In a March 1968 issue, *Newsweek* magazine proclaimed, "After three years of gradual escalation, President Johnson's strategy for Vietnam has run into a dead end."[64] And so had Johnson's political career.

President Nixon

Faced with growing criticism at home (even within his own Democratic Party) and an increasingly frustrating war abroad, Lyndon Johnson made a tough decision: He would not run for reelection. On March 31, 1968, Johnson told a nationwide television audience, "I shall not seek, and I will not accept, the nomination of my party for another term as your President."[65] Johnson's vice president, Hubert Humphrey, won the Democratic nomination for president after Robert Kennedy, the late President John F. Kennedy's brother and another candidate for the nomination, was assassinated. Humphrey promised that, if elected, he would end the war in Vietnam. But so did his Republican opponent, Richard M. Nixon.

Nixon, who had hunted for Communists in the 1950s and was vice president under Dwight D. Eisenhower, said he had a "secret plan" to end the Vietnam War, although he would not elaborate. Throughout most of the campaign, Nixon held a sizable lead in popularity over Humphrey. As the November elections approached, Humphrey began to narrow Nixon's lead. Then on October 31, less than a week before the election, President Johnson announced that he would halt the bombing of North Vietnam. This announcement helped Humphrey, but it was not enough to win

him the White House. Richard Nixon was elected the thirty-seventh president of the United States by a razor-thin margin of less than 1 percent of the votes.

Vietnamization

Richard Nixon took the oath of office on January 20, 1969. In his inaugural address, he expressed his hope that he could end the war in Vietnam: "I shall consecrate my

President Richard Nixon explains events in Vietnam during a nationally televised broadcast.

office, my energies, and all the wisdom I can summon, to the cause of peace among nations."[66] By this time it was becoming all too clear that the United States, despite its massive arsenal of weapons and hundreds of thousands of troops, would not be able to pull a victory out of the jungles and rice paddies of Vietnam. But to suddenly withdraw would cause the immediate loss of South Vietnam to the Communists and tell the Soviet Union and China that when the going gets rough, the United States gets out. So, as part of Nixon's plan to end the war, he began a policy of "Vietnamization." Under this plan, U.S. troops would gradually be withdrawn from Vietnam, to be re-placed by South Vietnamese soldiers who would continue the fight against a Communist takeover—with training and equipment provided by the United States. "I believed," Nixon later commented, "that what was important was to de-Americanize the war by training more effectively the Vietnamese troops—Vietnamization it was called. The only way you could really win the war would be for the South Vietnamese to develop the capability of winning themselves, so that they could defend [their country] once we left."[67]

In June 1969 Nixon announced that twenty-five thousand U.S. troops would be leaving Vietnam, with thousands more to

"Prague Spring"

Czechoslovakia had become a Communist nation in 1948, the result of a Soviet-sponsored overthrow of the democratic government. Over the next twenty years, opposition to the Communist rule, especially in the younger generation of Czechs, seethed just below the surface of daily life in the Eastern European nation. In late 1967, unrest began to fracture Communist unity, and in January 1968 Alexander Dubcek became first secretary of the Communist Party in Czechoslovakia. Dubcek was open to reforms in the Communist government and began abolishing censorship and relaxing government control of the economy. As quoted in Inside the Cold War: An Oral History by John Sharnik, Dubcek called his program of reforms "socialism with a human face."

The Soviet Union took a dim view of the "Prague Spring" reforms. In August, Communist Party secretary general Leonid Brezhnev, a member of the Soviet Union's ruling troika who was emerging as the real power in the country, ordered an invasion of the rebelling nation. Tanks and half a million Soviet troops poured across the border into Czechoslovakia. Dubcek was removed from power and imprisoned, and the liberal reforms of Prague Spring ended. Czechoslovakia was again firmly under the hard-line policies of the Soviet Union.

Several weeks after the invasion, Brezhnev explained his actions by saying that the Soviet Union had the right to intervene in any country where communism was in danger of being overthrown or was otherwise threatened. Because this plan was similar in intent to the Truman Doctrine (which stated that the United States would help any nation resist communism), it became known in the West as the Brezhnev Doctrine. But by whatever name it was known, it made clear the Soviet Union's intent to use force if necessary to keep straying nations in the Communist fold.

return home as the South Vietnamese took over more and
more of the fighting. There were
about 540,000 U.S. troops in Vietnam at the beginning of 1969;
Nixon hoped to reduce that
number to just over 200,000 by
the end of 1971. But as Nixon was
reducing ground troop strength
in Vietnam, he was beginning a
controversial bombing operation
on its neighbor, Cambodia.

Situated to the west of South
Vietnam, Cambodia had be-
come a haven for North Vietnamese troops, who established
supply depots and military bases,
or "sanctuaries," in the neutral
country. Communist soldiers could cross
the border into Vietnam, strike against
ARVN troops, and then escape back to
safety in Cambodia. In March 1969 President Nixon ordered the beginning of
bombing raids on the Cambodian sanctuaries. Conducted in strict secrecy because
Nixon feared increased protests at home
if Americans learned that their military
was bombing a neutral country, the campaign was designed not only to destroy
enemy installations in Cambodia but also
to force the North Vietnamese to negotiate seriously at peace talks that were then
going on in Paris.

*President Nixon wanted to decrease the number
of U.S. troops in Vietnam.*

Negotiating Peace

When Lyndon Johnson told the nation of
his decision not to run for reelection on

March 31, 1968, he also urged the North
Vietnamese to begin negotiating an end
to the Vietnam War. On May 10 prelimi-
nary talks were begun in Paris between
representatives of the United States and
North Vietnam. After prolonged hag-
gling over such matters as the shape of
the peace table, however, the talks
reached a stalemate.

On January 25, 1969, just five days after Richard Nixon entered the White
House, the Paris peace negotiations
were once more under way. These expanded talks included representatives of
South Vietnam and the National Liberation Front (NLF, the political arm of the
Vietcong) as well as the U.S. and North

Representatives from the United States, North Vietnam, and South Vietnam sign a peace treaty in Paris, ending the Vietnam War.

Vietnamese delegates who had already been negotiating. The North Vietnamese insisted on replacing South Vietnam's president, Nguyen Van Thieu, with a coalition government that would include the Vietcong, a provision that the United States would not agree to. In 1970 Henry Kissinger, Nixon's national security adviser, began secret talks with leaders of the North Vietnamese government. Nixon hoped these secret meetings would produce more results than the public talks. Kissinger would continue his secret negotiations for two years.

When negotiations broke down in December 1972, President Nixon resumed the bombing of North Vietnam in an effort to force the North Vietnamese representatives back to the peace table. The plan worked, and the talks resumed in January 1973. On January 27 the "Agreement on Ending the War and Restoring Peace in Vietnam" was signed by the delegates to the Paris talks. The longest war in U.S. history was finally over. It was one week after Richard Nixon's inauguration for a second term as president.

While the peace treaty signaled the end to U.S. involvement in the Vietnam War, it also led to the eventual collapse of a democratic South Vietnam. On March 29, 1973, the last U.S. combat troops left Vietnam, leaving only a few thousand civilians and a handful of guards at the U.S. embassy in Saigon. In June, Congress voted to deny further spending to help the South Vietnamese continue their fight against Communist North Vietnam. Without U.S. military and financial support, the ARVN could do little to stop the North Vietnamese army from overrunning South Vietnam. In April 1975, with the Communist troops approaching Saigon, helicopters began ferrying Americans and Vietnamese civilians from the U.S. embassy to the safety of ships waiting offshore. On April 30 the last helicopter lifted off the embassy roof. Aboard was the U.S. ambassador carrying the Stars and Stripes that had flown over the embassy. That same day, North Vietnamese troops captured Saigon, completing the Communist takeover of Vietnam.

In Vietnam, the United States lost the first war in its history and much of its idealism. More than fifty-seven thousand Americans had died fighting in jungles ten thousand miles away, and young Americans had been beaten and arrested in the streets at home. Because of the "credibility gap," Americans had lost faith that their government would always tell them the truth. And the reasons for fighting the war were increasingly unclear. It was obvious that the Cold War doctrine of containment had utterly failed in Vietnam. But America's leaders were still committed to containing communism. In fact, the nation was already turning its attention to its traditional Cold War rival, the Soviet Union, and to a new player in the game, the People's Republic of China.

★ Chapter 7 ★

Détente Gained and Lost

The Cold War was more than twenty years old in 1969, and during that time the strategic nuclear arsenals of the two superpowers—the United States and the Soviet Union—had grown to unprecedented sizes. Since 1967, the United States had deployed 1,054 intercontinental ballistic missiles (ICBMs) in underground silos and 656 missiles that could be launched from submarines (SLBMs). In addition, nearly 600 bombers stood ready to deliver nuclear bombs at a moment's notice. Although the Soviet Union had fewer bombers and submarine-launched missiles than the United States, it counted approximately 1,200 ICBMs in its nuclear stockpile. And the Soviets were building more than 300 additional ICBMs and submarine-launched missiles every year. The nuclear advantage that America had enjoyed in the early years of the Cold War was clearly over and could never be regained. An official study reported that "It was impossible to escape the conclusion that no conceivable American strategic program would give you the kind of superiority that you had in the 1950s."[68]

During the Cuban Missile Crisis in 1962, the world had narrowly averted a nuclear confrontation. But no one could be certain of the same outcome if another crisis brought the two nations head to head. Fortunately, their leaders were beginning to take steps to see that the unthinkable did not happen.

The Balance of Power

Both the United States and the Soviet Union knew that something had to be done to curb the escalating arms race. The two superpowers possessed enough nuclear weapons to destroy civilization many times over, and the only thing keeping the missiles from flying was a doctrine appropriately abbreviated MAD. The concept of "mutually assured destruction" stated that since both superpowers had enough weapons to inflict massive property damage and millions of human casualties, a first strike by either side would mean self-destruction as well, and would thus be pointless. The MAD doctrine created a delicate balance of power between the United States and the Soviet Union. Every increase in weaponry by one side had to be matched with a similar increase by the other to keep this crucial balance. And the prevailing ethic in weapons strategy was that more is better. As Robert McNamara, President Johnson's secretary of defense, explained, "There is a kind of mad momentum intrinsic to the development of all new nuclear weaponry. If a weapon system works—and works well—there is strong pressure from many directions to procure and deploy the weapon out of all proportion to the prudent level required."[69]

After President Johnson's 1967 meeting with Soviet premier Kosygin in Glassboro, New Jersey, hopes were high that additional talks might begin to make progress in disarmament. But the Soviet invasion of Czechoslovakia in August

Intercontinental ballistic missiles are paraded down Red Square in Moscow in 1969.

1968 shelved any plans for further negotiations. When Richard Nixon took office in January 1969, the Soviets once again expressed a willingness to resume arms limitation negotiations. The conferences that resulted, called the Strategic Arms Limitation Talks (SALT), produced the first agreements to limit the superpowers' nuclear arsenals and paved the way for the process of détente.

Détente

In his first inaugural address, President Richard Nixon spoke of the hopes he held for better relations between the United States and the Soviet Union: "After a period of confrontation, we are entering an era of negotiation."[70] It would be an irony of history if Nixon, the staunch anti-Communist of the 1950s, was the president who improved U.S. relations with the Communist world. But by 1972 that seemed to be just what was happening. This thaw in the Cold War was called détente, a French word meaning "the easing of tensions." The Soviets, too, welcomed détente. Georgi Arbatov, an adviser to Leonid Brezhnev, wrote, "This was actually one of the brightest periods, or maybe the brightest period, in postwar relations between the Soviet Union and the United States. A lot of things looked very possible at this time."[71] But although relations between the governments of the two nations were improving, the Cold War was taking a toll on the people living in the Soviet Union.

The cost of the massive military buildup that accompanied the Cold War had particularly hurt the Soviet Union. Its weak economy, a direct consequence of communism, made it difficult for the government to provide both missiles for the military and consumer goods for the ordinary citizen. The nation's farms could not produce enough grain to adequately feed the Soviet population. In contrast, the United States possessed an agricultural surplus, so in 1972 a deal was struck allowing the Soviet Union to purchase millions of tons of U.S. grain. The deal also stimulated many U.S. companies to seek out new markets in the Soviet Union. But while American grain helped feed millions of Soviet citizens, it resulted in higher prices for bread and other grain products at home. Some Americans began referring to the grain deal as the "great grain robbery."

The early 1970s also saw another advance in détente, this time in Berlin. In September 1971, the four major powers involved in Berlin (the United States, the Soviet Union, Great Britain, and France) signed an agreement to allow access from West Berlin into East Berlin and the German Democratic Republic (East Germany). Despite the continuing presence of the Berlin Wall, there was at last a small break in the fear and uncertainty that had gripped the city for more than twenty years. Further progress would be made, and in 1973 East and West Germany joined the United Nations.

President Nixon stands with Soviet leader Leonid Brezhnev on the White House balcony.

While the United States was forging stronger ties with the Soviet Union, it also recognized that it now had another Communist power to deal with. China, the most populous nation on earth and the largest Communist country, had entered the arena of Cold War politics.

Communist China

Since the Communist takeover by Chairman Mao Tse-tung in 1949, China had been through a series of programs designed to bring the ancient nation into the modern world. The "Great Leap For-

ward" in the late 1950s proposed sweeping changes aimed at modernizing Chinese society. These changes included improvements in agriculture, new public works projects, and the building of "backyard steel mills" in which ordinary citizens could produce steel for China's industrial needs. But the Great Leap Forward was a disaster, causing unprecedented

China's Cultural Revolution

Liang Heng, a writer who was a member of Mao Tse-tung's Red Guards in 1966, lived through the madness of the Cultural Revolution that swept across China. The following remembrance is taken from John Sharnik's book *Inside the Cold War: An Oral History.*

> The Cultural Revolution gradually, day by day, became crazy. Nobody really understood what was happening. I saw people use machine guns to shoot each other in the streets. Today this faction was wrong but tomorrow maybe they are right. Today you were right; maybe tomorrow you become a counterrevolutionary.

During China's Cultural Revolution, teenage boys and girls were enlisted into the Red Guards to enforce Mao Tse-Tung's Communist ideals and to punish all those who did not follow them.

Chairman Mao treated Chinese people as soldiers—all China as an army. He broke into the family structure. At that time, nobody went to school or college to study. Why? Because the slogan was very popular: "The more education and knowledge that you have, the more reactionary you are." So, no books, only Chairman Mao's books! The library was closed also. We had no school, and we were wandering the streets. . . .

My father, like most intellectuals, was sent into the countryside to do hard jobs, so I went to the countryside with my father. We often had no food. I was so hungry at night I went to the field to steal sweet potatoes.

We didn't know what happened outside of China. We only concerned ourselves with ourselves as a great people. Chairman Mao said the Chinese system was the number-one system in the world.

hardships and famine for millions of Chinese peasants.

The Great Proletarian Cultural Revolution, which lasted from 1966 to 1976, was Mao Tse-tung's attempt to improve Chinese society and rekindle the revolutionary spirit among his people. When the movement began, many top Communist Party officials were removed from their jobs. At the same time, millions of Chinese youth formed the Red Guards, a loosely organized semimilitary force whose purpose was to find and punish those deemed obstacles to China's revolutionary rebirth. The people identified by the Red Guards as obstacles eventually included anyone connected with traditional authority. The Red Guards held mass rallies, denouncing China's traditional ways and proclaiming Chairman Mao's words of wisdom. Soon they were sweeping across the country, destroying museums, libraries, and other historic structures, and murdering intellectuals, teachers, artists, and other innocent citizens.

Like the Great Leap Forward, the Cultural Revolution caused great hardships in China. Only when the country was on the verge of anarchy did Mao end the Cultural Revolution, leaving in its wake millions dead and the lives of many more disrupted forever.

China had experienced a stormy relationship with the Soviet Union during the decades after Mao converted his country to communism. The two nations had cemented their friendship in 1950 with the signing of a mutual assistance and defense agreement. The Soviet Union was allowed to station troops in China in return for economic aid and technical assistance from Soviet scientists and engineers. Soviet arms helped the Chinese support the North Korean army during the Korean War.

But by the late 1950s, the Chinese-Soviet friendship pact was unraveling. The two Communist giants were locked in a struggle to determine which would become the leader of the Communist world. Chinese leaders accused the Soviets of betraying communism and becoming too accommodating to the United States. The Soviets, in turn, withdrew their technical experts from China, leaving many important engineering projects unfinished. Soviet distrust of China grew as China became a nuclear power, detonating its first atomic bomb in 1964, followed by a hydrogen bomb just three years later. By 1969, Chinese and Soviet troops were fighting along their common border.

As the Chinese-Soviet split widened, China discovered that it had something in common with the United States: a fear of the Soviet Union's growing nuclear might. And in Washington, the time seemed right to try to improve American relations with China.

An Unprecedented Visit

During the summer of 1971 President Richard Nixon's national security adviser

Henry Kissinger was making a routine tour of Asia, a trip that included a stop in Pakistan. While visiting that nation's capital, Kissinger informed the press that he was not feeling well and that he would not be following his planned itinerary for a while. In fact, in the dead of night, Kissinger was secretly taken to an airport and whisked from Pakistan to the People's Republic of China. His clandestine mission was one of historic proportions: Kissinger was making arrangements for a visit to China by President Nixon.

After Kissinger completed his plans and returned to the United States, President Nixon spoke to the nation on television about his hopes for his upcoming visit to China: "I will undertake . . . a journey for peace, peace not just for our generation but for future generations on this earth we share together."[72]

Air Force One, the president's official airplane, touched down in Beijing on February 21, 1972, a cold, overcast winter day in the People's Republic of China. President Nixon was greeted by Chinese premier Zhou Enlai. Eighteen years earlier, Zhou had met

President Eisenhower's secretary of state John Foster Dulles, who had insulted Zhou by refusing to shake hands with the Communist leader. Now, Nixon and Zhou shook hands on the runway, a historic symbol of a new age of cooperation. As Nixon recalled in his memoirs, "When our hands met, one era ended and another began."[73]

Over the next week, Nixon had several meetings with Zhou Enlai, ate dinner with Mao Tse-tung (with Nixon skillfully using chopsticks), and spent time on sightseeing jaunts, which included a visit to the Great Wall of China. Through many hours of

President Nixon's historic meeting with Mao Tse-tung signaled new, friendlier relations between the two countries.

conversation with Zhou, Nixon became impressed with the premier's intelligence and energetic personality, as well as with his vast knowledge of history. "Unlike many world leaders and statesmen," Nixon later wrote, "who are completely absorbed in one particular cause or issue, Zhou En-lai was able to talk in broad terms about men and history."[74]

In the Shanghai Communiqué, a joint statement issued at the end of the trip, Nixon and Zhou frankly acknowledged the differences that remained between the two nations. But they vowed to work toward a peaceful coexistence and a normalization of relations between China and the United States. "We have been here a week," Nixon announced at the farewell banquet in Shanghai. "This was the week that changed the world."[75] Nixon was being overly enthusiastic, for no major agreements resulted from the president's trip to China. Indeed, it would take until 1979 for the United States to establish full diplomatic relations with the People's Republic of China. But Nixon's historic journey to the world's largest Communist nation was a crucial beginning.

The improving relations between the United States and both the Soviet Union and China seemed to be a hopeful sign that the antagonism between capitalist and Communist societies was finally easing. But within a few years détente would fall apart, leaving the world once more in the depths of the Cold War.

More Trouble in the Middle East

The Middle East crisis of 1956, which pitted Egypt against Israel, Great Britain, and France in a struggle for control of the Suez Canal, occurred when Richard Nixon was vice president under Dwight D. Eisenhower. As president, Nixon faced his own Middle East crisis in the fall of 1973.

Although the Six Day War of 1967 ended in an Israeli victory, six years later the Arab-Israeli disputes remained unresolved. On October 6, 1973, the Arab nations of Egypt and Syria launched a surprise attack against Israel. The day was Yom Kippur, the holiest day of the Jewish year, and the war became known as the Yom Kippur War. The attacking nations were friendly to the Soviet Union, and their forces were heavily armed with Soviet weapons. Soon, the Israeli army was on the run. Only with a massive emergency airlift of U.S. military supplies were the Israelis able to finally surround the Arab forces and threaten them with annihilation. The Soviet Union, fearing the imminent defeat of the Arab armies, prepared to send thousands of Soviet troops to the region.

For President Nixon, a Soviet military presence in the Middle East would be a dangerous and unacceptable escalation of a Cold War that had so recently seemed to be thawing. U.S. nuclear forces were put on alert for the first time since the Cuban Missile Crisis in 1962. Nixon warned Soviet premier

Israeli troops in battle during the Yom Kippur War. The Soviets and Americans supported opposing sides in the Middle East.

Brezhnev that deploying troops in the Middle East would jeopardize détente. Then he sent Henry Kissinger, who had been appointed secretary of state, to the Middle East to negotiate a cease-fire. Although peace was finally restored under the supervision of the United Nations, the Middle East remained a politically unstable part of the world. And despite the Soviet Union's role in escalating the conflict, détente survived the Yom Kippur War.

Nixon Resigns

President Nixon was angry that Premier Brezhnev, whose military advisers were in Egypt before the Yom Kippur War, had not alerted the United States to the impending hostilities. According to Cold War historian Michael Kort, "The Soviets had failed to warn the United States about Arab plans, thereby, at least from the American point of view, violating the spirit of détente."[76] But despite Soviet actions, the president was not ready to give up on détente just yet.

In late June and early July 1974 Nixon and Brezhnev held a summit meeting in Moscow, during which the two leaders signed a limited underground nuclear test ban agreement. The most important understanding to come out of the summit, Nixon wrote in his memoirs, was "the oral agreement I made with Brezhnev for a mini-summit before the end of 1974 for the purpose of reaching agreement on limitations of offensive nuclear weapons."[77] His plans, however, would never be realized. For more than a year, Nixon had been preoccupied with a domestic political scandal,

suspected of involvement in the coverup of a politically motivated burglary at the Watergate hotel in Washington. Faced with certain impeachment, on August 8, 1974, Richard Nixon resigned as president of the United States. America's Cold War policy would continue under Nixon's successor, Gerald R. Ford.

Détente's Zenith

President Ford announced that he wanted to get the United States past the Watergate affair and back to the important matters concerning the nation. One of those matters was the Cold War relations between the United States and the Soviet Union, and the continuation of détente. In November Ford met with Brezhnev at Vladivostok in the Soviet Union, where the two leaders hammered out a

Ping-Pong and Politics

The first hint that China was willing to consider improving relations with the United States occurred at an improbable event: an international Ping-Pong tournament. In April 1971 the U.S. Ping-Pong team was playing in a tournament in Japan, competing against teams from other countries, including the People's Republic of China. At the conclusion of the tournament, Chinese officials invited the U.S. team to visit China and play the Chinese team there. It was a remarkable invitation, for no American had officially visited China since the Communist revolution in 1949. The Americans went to China the next month and although they lost to the Chinese team, they received a warm welcome to the People's Republic of China. A year later, the Chinese Ping-Pong team would be invited for a similar visit to the United States.

This "Ping-Pong diplomacy," as it was called, signaled the beginning of a thaw in U.S.-Chinese relations. In June 1971 President Nixon lifted a trade embargo against China that had been in place for more than two decades; later in the year the United States would drop its long-held objection to China's membership in the United Nations. Ping-Pong diplomacy also paved the way for a secret trip to China that summer by Henry Kissinger. Kissinger met with Chinese premier Zhou Enlai, who admitted that the Cultural Revolution had severely weakened his nation's economy and that a new relationship with the United States would be welcomed. By the end of Kissinger's visit, details had been worked out for a historic visit to China by President Nixon.

framework for a proposed new arms limitation treaty to be known as SALT II. Years of negotiations lay ahead before the treaty would be ready for ratification. But the Vladivostok summit conference showed that the two superpowers still realized the value of cooperation in the nuclear arena.

Another encouraging sign that détente was working came on August 1, 1975, when thirty-five nations signed the Helsinki Accords. The scene was the conclusion of the Conference on Security and Cooperation in Europe, which was attended by President Ford, Premier Brezhnev, and the leaders of every major European country. The Helsinki Accords officially recognized the borders of Europe's nations as they had been established after World War II. In addition, the signers of the accords pledged to respect basic human rights, calling for "the effective exercise of civil, political, economic, social, cultural, and other rights and freedoms all of which derive from the inherent dignity of the human person and are essential for his free and full development."[78] The agreement was a victory for the Soviet Union, which received validation of the Eastern European borders it had essentially created by force after the war, in return for its promise to respect basic human rights. Whether it would keep that promise would be watched closely by the United States and other Western nations.

The year 1975 was the high point of détente, with cooperation between the United States and the Soviet Union extending even into outer space. In July, U.S. astronauts and Soviet cosmonauts came together in the first joint international space venture. The docking of an American Apollo and a Soviet Soyuz spacecraft more than one hundred miles above the earth symbolized a relationship between the two nations that would have been unthinkable just a decade before. But just as astronauts must eventually return from space, so too did the good feelings of détente ultimately fall to earth—for the United States and the Soviet Union each had a different concept of détente. While the United States viewed détente as an un-

President Nixon and his wife, Pat, stroll along the White House lawn on his last day in office. Gerald Ford (far left) became president upon Nixon's resignation.

SALT

The Strategic Arms Limitations Talks (SALT) I were a series of seven arms control negotiations held between the United States and the Soviet Union over a period of two and a half years. The sessions lasted about three months each and were located alternately in the cities of Helsinki, Finland, and Vienna, Austria.

The discussions ranged from defining which missiles would be the subject of negotiations to whether U.S. bombers based in Europe were to be included in any arms reduction agreement. When the main talks reached an impasse in 1971, secret back-channel negotiations between National Security Adviser Kissinger and Soviet ambassador Anatoly Dobrynin were able to break the deadlock.

On May 26, 1972, President Richard Nixon and Soviet general secretary Leonid Brezhnev concluded SALT I with the signing of two agreements. These agreements restricted the deployment of antiballistic missile systems for an unlimited period of time and froze the number of offensive missiles for five years. The numbers of submarine-launched ballistic missiles and the submarines that carry them were also limited by the agreements.

In 1974 President Gerald Ford and Premier Brezhnev agreed to proceed with another round of arms limitation talks, called SALT II. But little progress was made during Ford's administration, and by 1977 it was up to President Jimmy Carter to continue the talks. At first, the negotiations did not go well. When Carter attempted to link the improvement of Soviet human rights with the nuclear arms negotiations, Brezhnev merely repeated the Soviet position that human rights was an internal concern. But after several years of negotiations, the SALT II treaty was finally signed in June 1979. The agreement placed limits on the number of offensive nuclear missiles and launch facilities each nation could have. Although SALT II was one of the bright spots of Carter's presidency, many Americans felt the treaty gave the Soviet Union too many advantages and that Carter was being "soft" on communism. Whether this criticism was justified or not ultimately did not matter. The United States never ratified the SALT II treaty as a way of protesting Soviet expansionism in Afghanistan.

derstanding of worldwide scope, the Soviet Union saw it only as adherence to narrowly defined U.S.-Soviet agreements. So, as the United States struggled to put the Vietnam War and the Watergate scandal behind it, the Soviet Union was looking for new areas of the globe to expand communism.

By 1976, America's bicentennial year, the nation was in the mood for a change. Americans went to the polls in November and elected James Earl Carter, a likable but little-known peanut farmer from Georgia, as the thirty-ninth president of the United States.

Human Rights

Jimmy Carter was a good-natured man who, as former governor of Georgia, considered himself an outsider when it came to the power plays and political cronyism of Washington. He saw his administration as one that would reestablish honesty and virtue in the White House. As president, Carter conducted the Cold War not with back-channel diplomacy

Jimmy Carter and his family greet the crowd at his 1977 presidential inauguration.

and nuclear brinkmanship but by extolling the importance of human rights for all people around the world. "I wanted the American people to understand," Carter later recalled, "that I, as their President, would no longer predicate what we decided on hundreds of issues on an inordinate fear or concern about the Soviet Union."[79]

Taking the Helsinki Accords as his foundation, Carter aimed his human rights criticism directly at Moscow. He vo-

cally supported Soviet dissidents who denounced their government. Carter also tried to force the Soviets to improve the treatment of their citizens by imposing embargoes on computers and other exports destined for the Soviet Union. These acts angered Soviet premier Brezhnev, who declared that Carter was interfering in the internal affairs of the Soviet Union. But despite their differences on human rights, in June 1979 Carter and Brezhnev were able to cooperate in SALT II, which produced a new arms control treaty. However, this treaty never went into effect because the United States refused to ratify it in response to new Soviet intervention, and Communist expansion, in yet another part of the world.

Afghanistan

The ancient land of Afghanistan lies at the crossroads of the Middle East, between the Soviet Union, Pakistan, China, and Iran. It is a nation of diverse ethnic groups and a rugged topography of steep mountains and barren plains. After a revolution in 1978, Afghanistan became a Marxist state backed by the Soviet Union. From the beginning, the new regime was unpopular and soon the local Muslim tribes rebelled. With the Marxist government on the verge of collapse, the Soviet Union sent thirty thousand Red Army troops to Afghanistan in December 1979. It was the first time that the Soviet army had been deployed outside the Soviet sphere of influence since the end of World War II. Eventually, more than 100,000 troops would fight a futile war that would later become known as the Soviet Union's Vietnam.

President Carter's reaction to the Soviet troops in Afghanistan was swift and angry: "An attempt by any force to gain control of the Persian Gulf region will be regarded as an assault on the vital interests of the United States."[80] Carter asked

Fellow soldiers aid a wounded Afghan fighter. Many Muslim tribes in Afghanistan rebelled against Marxist control.

Congress for a 15 percent increase in the U.S. military budget, cut grain shipments to the Soviet Union, and refused to allow U.S. athletes to attend the 1980 Olympic Games in Moscow. In a final act of protest, Carter withdrew the SALT II agreement from consideration by the Senate. As the decade of the 1970s came to an end, arms control, and with it détente, was dead.

A Cold Future

For thirty-five years, two nations had struggled through a conflict unlike any other in history. The Cold War began even before World War II had ended. It fought new wars, built new weapons of awesome destructive power, and forged new political alliances. It survived a missile crisis that propelled an anxious world to the brink of annihilation and, thankfully, back again. The Cold War stretched from the frozen landscape of Korea to the opulent locales of summit conferences to the very heights of outer space. And during it all, the world watched and waited as the United States and the Soviet Union struggled to come to terms with each other's ideology.

For Americans, the Cold War was the constant background of daily life, not comforting like a familiar song but a monotonous undertone that was always present, only occasionally disrupting routine activities. Americans learned to live with it, for in truth, there was nothing they could do to end it. As the decade of the 1980s began, it seemed as if the Cold War might go on forever. No one could know that the end was perhaps closer than they dared hope.

★ Notes ★

Introduction: A Conflict of Ideas

1. Karl Marx, "A Critique of the Gotha Programme, 1875," *Marxist Internet Archive.* www.marxists.org.

Chapter 1: Origins of the Cold War

2. Quoted in Ralph B. Levering, *The Cold War, 1945–1972.* Arlington Heights, IL: Harlan Davidson, 1982, p. 5.
3. Quoted in Levering, *The Cold War,* p. 5.
4. Quoted in Jim Bishop, *FDR's Last Year: April 1944–April 1945.* New York: William Morrow, 1974, p. 600.
5. Quoted in David McCullough, *Truman.* New York: Simon and Schuster, 1992, p. 372.
6. Quoted in McCullough, *Truman,* p. 376.
7. Quoted in McCullough, *Truman,* p. 421.
8. Quoted in Keith Wheeler, *The Fall of Japan.* Alexandria, VA: Time-Life Books, 1983, p. 32.
9. Quoted in McCullough, *Truman,* p. 416.
10. McCullough, *Truman,* p. 432.
11. Quoted in McCullough, *Truman,* p. 442.
12. Quoted in McCullough, *Truman,* p. 451.
13. Quoted in Wheeler, *The Fall of Japan,* p. 172.
14. Quoted in Martin Walker, *The Cold War: A History.* New York: Henry Holt, 1994, p. 29.
15. Joseph Stalin, "Stalin Addresses His Constituents," *Soviet News,* no. 1370, February 11, 1946. www.tasc.ac.uk.
16. George F. Kennan, *Memoirs, 1925–1950.* Boston: Little, Brown, 1967, p. 557.

Chapter 2: The Cold War Begins

17. Quoted in John Sharnik, *Inside the Cold War: An Oral History.* New York: Arbor House, 1987, p. 29.
18. Quoted in McCullough, *Truman,* p. 541.
19. Quoted in McCullough, *Truman,* p. 548.
20. Quoted in McCullough, *Truman,* p. 548.
21. Quoted in McCullough, *Truman,* p. 563.
22. Quoted in Melvyn P. Leffler, *The Specter*

of Communism: The United States and the Origins of the Cold War, 1917–1953. New York: Hill and Wang, 1994, p. 65.

23. Quoted in Michael Kort, *The Columbia Guide to the Cold War*. New York: Columbia University Press, 1998, p. 28.

24. Quoted in McCullough, *Truman*, p. 630.

25. Quoted in Sharnik, *Inside the Cold War*, p. 48.

26. Quoted in Office of the Historian, U.S. Department of State, *The Origins of NATO: The North Atlantic Treaty Organization*, Publication No. 10617, 1999. www.state.gov.

27. Quoted in Sharnik, *Inside the Cold War*, pp. 56–57.

28. Quoted in McCullough, *Truman*, p. 772.

Chapter 3: Cold War Battlefronts

29. Quoted in McCullough, *Truman*, pp. 776–777.

30. Harry G. Summers Jr., *Korean War Almanac*. New York: Facts On File, 1990, p. xiv.

31. Quoted in Sharnik, *Inside the Cold War*, p. 70.

32. Quoted in McCullough, *Truman*, p. 759.

33. Quoted in Thomas C. Reeves, *The Life and Times of Joe McCarthy*. New York: Stein and Day, 1982, p. 224.

34. Quoted in Reeves, *The Life and Times of Joe McCarthy*, p. 631.

35. Quoted in G.J.A. O'Toole, *Honorable Treachery: A History of U.S. Intelligence, Espionage, and Covert Action from the American Revolution to the CIA*. New York: Atlantic Monthly Press, 1991, p. 462.

Chapter 4: The Cold War Expands

36. Quoted in James L. Stokesbury, *A Short History of the Korean War*. New York: William Morrow, 1988, p. 236.

37. Dwight D. Eisenhower, *Mandate for Change: The White House Years 1953–1956*. Garden City, NY: Doubleday, 1963, pp. 144–45.

38. Quoted in Sharnik, *Inside the Cold War*, p. 95.

39. Quoted in Sharnik, *Inside the Cold War*, p. 97.

40. Eisenhower, *Mandate for Change*, p. 451.

41. Quoted in David Halberstam, *The Fifties*. New York: Villard Books, 1993, p. 625.

42. Quoted in Sharnik, *Inside the Cold War*, p. 104.

43. Quoted in Sharnik, *Inside the Cold War*, p. 118.

44. Dwight D. Eisenhower, *Waging Peace: The White House Years 1956–1961*. Garden City, NY: Doubleday, 1965, p. 551.

Chapter 5: To the Brink of War

45. Quoted in Theodore Sorensen, *Kennedy*. New York: Harper and Row, 1965, p. 245.

46. Quoted in Sorensen, *Kennedy,* p. 246.

47. Quoted in Sharnik, *Inside the Cold War,* p. 143.

48. Quoted in Dino A. Brugioni, *Eyeball to Eyeball: The Inside Story of the Cuban Missile Crisis.* New York: Random House, 1991, p. 186.

49. Quoted in Brugioni, *Eyeball to Eyeball,* p. 200.

50. Quoted in Sorensen, *Kennedy,* p. 671.

51. Quoted in Brugioni, *Eyeball to Eyeball,* p. 231.

52. Quoted in Laurence Chang and Peter Kornbluh, eds., *The Cuban Missile Crisis: A National Security Archive Documents Reader.* New York: New Press, 1992, p. 150.

53. Quoted in Chang and Kornbluh, *The Cuban Missile Crisis,* p. 370.

54. Quoted in Chang and Kornbluh, *The Cuban Missile Crisis,* p. 370.

55. Quoted in Chang and Kornbluh, *The Cuban Missile Crisis,* p. 230.

56. Quoted in Chang and Kornbluh, *The Cuban Missile Crisis,* p. 232.

Chapter 6: The Vietnam Era

57. Quoted in William Appleman Williams et al., eds., *America in Vietnam: A Documentary History.* Garden City, NY: Anchor Press, 1985, p. 237.

58. Quoted in Stanley Karnow, *Vietnam: A History.* New York: Viking Press, 1983, p. 169.

59. Quoted in Karnow, *Vietnam,* p. 426.

60. Quoted in Robert Dallek, *Flawed Giant: Lyndon Johnson and His Times 1961–1973.* New York: Oxford University Press, 1998, p. 435.

61. Quoted in Dallek, *Flawed Giant,* p. 436.

62. Quoted in Dallek, *Flawed Giant,* p. 435.

63. Quoted in Karnow, *Vietnam,* p. 514.

64. Quoted in Clark Dougan, Stephen Weiss, and the Editors of Boston Publishing, *1968.* Boston: Boston Publishing, 1983, p. 70.

65. Quoted in Dallek, *Flawed Giant,* p. 529.

66. Quoted in Stephen E. Ambrose, *Nixon: The Triumph of a Politician, 1962–1972.* New York: Simon and Schuster, 1989, p. 244.

67. Quoted in Sharnik, *Inside the Cold War,* p. 220.

Chapter 7: Détente Gained and Lost

68. Quoted in Ambrose, *Nixon,* p. 289.

69. Quoted in Roger P. Labrie, ed., *SALT Handbook: Key Documents and Issues 1972–1979.* Washington, DC: American Enterprise Institute for Public Policy Research, 1979, p. 8.

70. Quoted in Kort, *The Columbia Guide to the Cold War,* p. 63.

71. Quoted in Sharnik, *Inside the Cold War,* p. 239.

72. Quoted in Ambrose, *Nixon,* p. 453.

73. Richard M. Nixon, *The Memoirs of Richard Nixon.* New York: Grosset and Dunlap, 1978, p. 559.

74. Nixon, *The Memoirs of Richard Nixon,* p. 577.

75. Quoted in Ambrose, *Nixon,* p. 517.

76. Kort, *The Columbia Guide to the Cold War,* p. 69.

77. Nixon, *The Memoirs of Richard Nixon,* p. 1,036.

78. Quoted in Civitas International, *Helsinki Accords.* www.civnet.org.

79. Quoted in Sharnik, *Inside the Cold War,* p. 275.

80. Quoted in Sharnik, *Inside the Cold War,* p. 301.

★ Chronology of Events ★

1945
February 4–12: The Yalta Conference.
July 16: The first atomic bomb is exploded in New Mexico.
July 17–August 2: The Potsdam Conference.

1947
March 12: President Truman announces the Truman Doctrine.
June 5: The Marshall Plan is proposed.

1948
June 24: The Berlin Blockade begins.
June 28: The Berlin Airlift begins.

1949
April 4: The North Atlantic Treaty Organization (NATO) is formed.
May 12: The Berlin Blockade ends.
October 1: The People's Republic of China is formed by Mao Tse-tung.

1950
June 25: The Korean War begins.
November 25–26: Chinese Communist troops in Korea stage massive attack against UN forces.

1953
March 5: Joseph Stalin dies.

July 27: The armistice ending the Korean War is signed.

1955
May 14: The Warsaw Pact is formed.
August 4: The first U-2 spy plane flies over Russia.

1956
October 23: The Hungarian Revolution begins.
October 29: The Suez Crisis begins.

1957
October 4: The Soviet Union launches *Sputnik,* the first artificial satellite.

1960
May 1: A U-2 spy plane is shot down over the Soviet Union.
May 16: The Paris summit meeting is canceled.

1961
April 17: The Bay of Pigs invasion begins.
August 13: Construction of the Berlin Wall begins.

1962
October 14–28: The Cuban Missile Crisis.

1963

August 5: A limited nuclear test ban treaty is signed.

November 22: President Kennedy is assassinated in Dallas.

1964

August 7: Congress passes the Gulf of Tonkin Resolution, opening the way for a U.S. combat role in Vietnam.

1968

May 10–13: The United States and North Vietnam begin peace talks.

August 20: Soviet troops invade Czechoslovakia.

1969

U.S. troop strength in Vietnam peaks at more than 543,000.

1972

February 21: President Nixon begins a historic trip to China.

1973

January 27: A peace agreement is signed in Paris; U.S. combat involvement in Vietnam ends.

1974

June 28: Nixon-Brezhnev summit meeting begins in Moscow.

1975

April 30: Saigon falls to Communists, ending the Vietnam War.

August 1: The Helsinki Accords are signed by thirty-five nations.

1979

January 1: The United States and the People's Republic of China establish diplomatic relations.

December 27: Soviet troops invade Afghanistan.

☆ For Further Reading ☆

Rafaela Ellis, *The Central Intelligence Agency.* New York: Chelsea House, 1988. This book is an easy-to-read history of American espionage from the forerunners of the CIA to present-day covert operations. Includes a short glossary of espionage terms and a selected reference list.

Doris M. Epler, *The Berlin Wall: How It Rose and Why It Fell.* Brookfield, CT: Millbrook Press, 1992. This book presents the story of the Berlin Wall from its construction in 1961 to its destruction twenty-eight years later. Illustrated with black-and-white photographs, the book includes a chronology of the Berlin Wall, a bibliography, and a recommended reading list.

Kathlyn Gay and Martin Gay, *The Korean War.* New York: Twenty-First Century Books, 1996. This brief overview of the Korean War features quotes from people who lived through it. It is illustrated with black-and-white photographs and includes a list of books and videos about the war.

Catherine Hester Gow, *The Cuban Missile Crisis.* San Diego: Lucent Books, 1997. A complete account of the Cold War event that brought the world closer than it has ever been to a nuclear holocaust. Includes a reading list and numerous photographs.

Stuart A. Kallen, *The 1950s.* San Diego: Lucent Books, 1999. This book takes a look at life in the United States during the 1950s, the first full decade of the Cold War. The author chronicles '50s culture in a lively, informative style and includes numerous black-and-white photos.

Michael G. Kort, *China Under Communism.* Brookfield, CT: Millbrook Press, 1994. This book traces the history of China in the twentieth century, with emphasis on events that are often misunderstood by Westerners. China's Communist revolution and its subsequent turbulent years are explored.

——, *The Cold War.* Brookfield, CT: Millbrook Press, 1994. This book presents a concise history of the Cold War in a readable style, illustrated with numerous photographs. The author devotes chapters to such Cold War crises as the Korean War, the Cuban Missile Crisis, and Vietnam.

Harry Nickelson, *Vietnam.* San Diego: Lucent Books, 1989. A comprehensive examination of the Vietnam War that provides answers to questions such as why did America get involved in Vietnam, why did it decide to leave, and what caused South Vietnam to ultimately fall to communism?

Edward Rice, *Marx, Engels, and the Workers of the World*. New York: Four Winds Press, 1977. This book recounts the life and ideas of Karl Marx, who, with his collaborator Friedrich Engels, laid the economic and political foundations of communism.

James A. Warren, *Cold War: The American Crusade Against World Communism 1945–1991*. New York: Lothrop, Lee, and Shepard, 1996. This book provides a comprehensive and easy-to-read history of the Cold War for young adults. The author chronicles the origins, major events, and end of the nearly fifty-year-long conflict. Includes a chronology of the Cold War years.

Scott Westerfeld, *The Berlin Airlift*. Englewood Cliffs, NJ: Silver Burdett, 1989. This illustrated book tells the story of the Berlin Airlift, beginning with a brief overview of World War II and the forces that led to the partitioning of Germany. An afterword summarizes the Cold War and Berlin's role as a symbol of a divided world.

⋆ Works Consulted ⋆

Books

Stephen E. Ambrose, *Nixon: The Triumph of a Politician, 1962–1972.* New York: Simon and Schuster, 1989. Ambrose, a renowned historian, traces the life of Richard Nixon from his "withdrawal" from public life in 1962 to his election for a second term as president of the United States.

Jim Bishop, *FDR's Last Year: April 1944–April 1945.* New York: William Morrow, 1974. This book, based on extensive interviews with people close to Roosevelt, creates an intimate portrait of FDR in the last year of his life and chronicles world events at the end of World War II.

Dino A. Brugioni, *Eyeball to Eyeball: The Inside Story of the Cuban Missile Crisis.* New York: Random House, 1991. The author, a CIA official who supervised the preparation of reconnaissance photos during the Cuban Missile Crisis, gives an insider's account of the dangerous days of the crisis in October 1962.

Laurence Chang and Peter Kornbluh, eds., *The Cuban Missile Crisis: A National Security Archive Documents Reader.* New York: New Press, 1992. This book reproduces memos, official reports, and meeting transcripts that trace the course of the Cuban Missile Crisis.

Robert Dallek, *Flawed Giant: Lyndon Johnson and His Times 1961–1973.* New York: Oxford University Press, 1998. This book (volume 2 of a two-volume biography) takes a detailed, behind-the-scenes look at the contradictions that made up President Johnson.

Clark Dougan, Stephen Weiss, and the Editors of Boston Publishing, *1968.* Boston: Boston Publishing, 1983. This volume in The Vietnam Experience series takes an in-depth look at 1968, a critical year in war both at home and abroad.

Dwight D. Eisenhower, *Mandate for Change: The White House Years 1953–1956.* Garden City, NY: Doubleday, 1963. In the first volume of Eisenhower's memoirs of his White House years, the former president recalls the events of his first term in office.

———, *Waging Peace: The White House Years 1956–1961.* Garden City, NY: Doubleday, 1965. In this second volume of Eisenhower's memoirs, he describes the ever-increasing complexity of the Cold War world and his reactions to various world crises.

Griffin Fariello, *Red Scare: Memories of the American Inquisition.* New York: W.W. Norton, 1995. This book examines the Communist witch-hunts and blacklists of the 1940s and '50s through the words of actors, writers, and intellectuals who were persecuted.

Lawrence Freedman, *Kennedy's Wars: Berlin, Cuba, Laos, and Vietnam.* New York: Oxford University Press, 2000. Traces the various world crises faced by President John F. Kennedy during his short term in office.

David Halberstam, *The Fifties.* New York: Villard Books, 1993. A popular and thorough history of 1950s' society, written by a Pulitzer Prize–winning author.

Stanley Karnow, *Vietnam: A History.* New York: Viking Press, 1983. Journalist Stanley Karnow wrote this book as a companion volume to the PBS series *Vietnam: A Television History.* It chronicles Vietnam's history from its years as a French colony to the fall of Saigon.

George F. Kennan, *Memoirs, 1925–1950.* Boston: Little, Brown, 1967. The personal recollections of twenty-five years in the author's diplomatic career. Kennan relates his personal encounters and the important events that shaped U.S. foreign relations during the period.

Henry Kissinger, *Years of Renewal.* New York: Simon and Schuster, 1999. This second volume of Kissinger's two-volume memoirs covers the period from the downfall of Richard Nixon through the presidency of Gerald Ford.

Michael Kort, *The Columbia Guide to the Cold War.* New York: Columbia University Press, 1998. This comprehensive reference guide to the Cold War includes a narrative history, a dictionary of names and terms, a chronology of the Cold War years, and a list of resources in all media (print, film and video, CD-ROMs, and websites).

Roger P. Labrie, ed., *SALT Handbook: Key Documents and Issues 1972–1979.* Washington, DC: American Enterprise Institute for Public Policy Research, 1979. This book presents the history of the Strategic Arms Limitation Talks through their most important documents, treaties, agreements, and transcripts of congressional testimony.

Melvyn P. Leffler, *The Specter of Communism: The United States and the Origins of the Cold War, 1917–1953.* New York: Hill and Wang, 1994. The author traces the ideological battle between the United States and the Soviet Union and shows how Stalin's unpredictability and brutality fueled anxieties in the United States.

Ralph B. Levering, *The Cold War, 1945–1972.* Arlington Heights, IL: Harlan Davidson, 1982. A general overview of the Cold War years up to 1972.

David McCullough, *Truman.* New York: Simon and Schuster, 1992. The author won the Pulitzer Prize for this exhaustive and highly readable biography of President Harry S. Truman.

Richard M. Nixon, *The Memoirs of Richard Nixon.* New York: Grosset and Dunlap,

1978. In this autobiography, Nixon tells of his childhood in California and recounts the ups and downs of a political career that spanned nearly thirty years.

G.J.A. O'Toole, *Honorable Treachery: A History of U.S. Intelligence, Espionage, and Covert Action from the American Revolution to the CIA*. New York: Atlantic Monthly Press, 1991. A thorough history of American espionage written by a former employee of the CIA.

Robert Payne, *The Rise and Fall of Stalin*. New York: Simon and Schuster, 1965. This biography covers the years of Stalin's greatest power and reveals not only Stalin the politician but Stalin the man: ruthless, cunning, and cruel.

Geoffrey Perret, *Eisenhower*. New York: Random House, 1999. The author of this in-depth biography calls upon recently available material to bring the World War II general and U.S. president to life. Perret shows how Ike's military career prepared him to lead the nation during the prosperous yet dangerous 1950s.

Francis Gary Powers, with Curt Gentry, *Operation Overflight: The U-2 Spy Pilot Tells His Story for the First Time*. New York: Holt, Rinehart, and Winston, 1970. Powers, the pilot whose U-2 was shot down over the Soviet Union in 1960, describes the ill-fated flight, his captivity, and his eventual release from a Soviet prison.

Thomas C. Reeves, *The Life and Times of Joe McCarthy*. New York: Stein and Day, 1982. The author uses interviews with people who knew McCarthy and previously unavailable information to create a thorough biography of one of the most controversial figures of the 1950s.

Arthur M. Schlesinger, *A Thousand Days: John F. Kennedy in the White House*. Boston: Houghton Mifflin, 1965. A personal memoir of the Kennedy presidency by a man who served as special assistant to the president.

John Sharnik, *Inside the Cold War: An Oral History*. New York: Arbor House, 1987. The author, a television news producer, gives unique insight into the Cold War years with extensive quotes from people who lived through, and in many instances had an important effect on, the Cold War.

Gerard Smith, *Doubletalk: The Story of SALT I*. Garden City, NY: Doubleday, 1980. The story of the first Strategic Arms Limitation Talks, as told by America's chief negotiator.

Theodore Sorensen, *Kennedy*. New York: Harper and Row, 1965. Sorensen, Kennedy's special counsel, presents an insider's look at JFK and his administration.

James L. Stokesbury, *A Short History of the Korean War*. New York: William Morrow, 1988. A concise history of the Korean "police action" by an author whose works include histories of World War I and World War II. The importance of U.S. naval and air operations in Korea is highlighted.

Harry G. Summers Jr., *Korean War Almanac*. New York: Facts On File, 1990. A three-part examination of the Korean War: Part 1 is an overview of the war; part 2, a wartime chronology; and part 3, an alphabetical compilation of articles on the people, places, weapons, and battles of the war.

Ferenc Morton Szasz, *The Day the Sun Rose Twice*. Albuquerque: University of New Mexico Press, 1984. This book tells the story behind the development of the world's first atomic bomb and its test detonation in the New Mexico desert.

Rudy Tomedi, *No Bugles, No Drums: An Oral History of the Korean War*. New York: John Wiley & Sons, 1993. First-person accounts of the Korean War by the soldiers who fought it.

Ann Tusa and John Tusa, *The Berlin Airlift*. New York: Atheneum, 1988. This dramatic account of the Berlin Airlift tells of the hardships endured by the people of Berlin and of the heroic airlift pilots who flew around the clock to bring relief to the besieged city.

Martin Walker, *The Cold War: A History*. New York: Henry Holt, 1994. The author, an award-winning political commentator, writes a thorough history of the Cold War from Yalta to the fall of the Berlin Wall.

William Westmoreland, *A Soldier Reports*. Garden City, NY: Doubleday, 1976. An inside account of the Vietnam War by the man who was field commander from 1964 to 1968 and army chief of staff from 1968 to 1972.

Keith Wheeler, *The Fall of Japan*. Alexandria, VA: Time-Life Books, 1983. A volume in the Time-Life series World War II, this book presents the events leading up to the atomic bombing of Japan and its subsequent surrender. Includes numerous black-and-white photographs.

William Appleman Williams, et al., eds., *America in Vietnam: A Documentary History*. Garden City, NY: Anchor Press, 1985. A collection of documents tracing the Vietnam War from before World War II to South Vietnam's ultimate fall to the Communists. Introductory essays by the authors place the documents in their historical contexts.

Vladislav Zubok and Constantine Pleshakov, *Inside the Kremlin's Cold War*. Cambridge, MA: Harvard University Press, 1996. An examination of the Cold War years from the Soviet perspective.

Internet Sources

Civitas International, The Helsinki Accords, www.civnet.org. This worldwide nongovernmental civic education organization sponsors an online resource site for teachers, curriculum designers, scholars, policy makers, and journalists.

Karl Marx, "A Critique of the Gotha Programme, 1875," *Marxist Internet Archive*. www.marxists.org. This website is an online repository of Marxist writings compiled by volunteers from all over the world; it also includes a history of Marxism.

Office of the Historian, U.S. Department of State, *The Origins of NATO: The North Atlantic Treaty Organization,* Publication No. 10617, 1999. www.state.gov. This document provides a comprehensive history of NATO that includes a chronology, photographs, and many quotes.

Joseph Stalin, "Stalin Addresses His Constituents," *Soviet News,* no. 1370. www.tasc.ac.uk. This website, for Trinity and All Saints College (University of Leeds) in Horsforth, England, includes many texts for a humanities course syllabus.

☆ Index ☆

★ Picture Credits ★

★ About the Author ★

Craig E. Blohm has been writing magazine articles on historical subjects for children for more than fifteen years. He has also written for social studies textbooks and has conducted workshops in writing history for children. A native of Chicago, he has worked for more than twenty-five years in the field of television production, serving in various positions including production manager, writer, producer, and director. He is currently the television and radio production coordinator at Purdue University Calumet in Hammond, Indiana. He and his wife, Desiree, live in Tinley Park, Illinois, and have two sons, Eric and Jason.